Never Try To Arouse Erotic Love Until —

Never Try To Arouse Erotic Love Until –

The Song of Songs, in Critique of Solomon: A Study Companion

CALVIN G. SEERVELD

Dordt College Press

Consulting Editor: John H. Kok
Cover by Willem Hart
Layout by Carla Goslinga

Printed in the United States of America.

Dordt College Press   www.dordt.edu/DCPcatalog
498 Fourth Avenue NE
Sioux Center, Iowa 51250
ISBN: 978-1-940567-20-4

The Library of Congress Cataloging-in-Publication Data is on file with the Library of Congress, Washington, D.C.
Library of Congress Control Number: 2018942829

Dedicated to the women and men
who are or have been friends with me,
and those who touched my life for good
at one time or another that I dearly remember.

"I have become conscious lately, again and again, of how I think and experience things as the Older Testament does. In the past few months I have also been reading more Older Testament than Newer Testament passages.

"Only when a person knows keenly the Unspeakableness of the Name of God, may one then dare carefully take the Name of Jesus Christ on one's lips. Only when a person comes to love this life and the earth so much that with the termination of your life everything seems to be lost and have come to an end, may you then have faith in the resurrection of the dead and a new world that is coming. Only when a person lets the law of God hover over you to be obeyed, may you indeed once in a while speak of grace; and only when the anger and wrath of God remains firmly binding as a sure reality over God's enemies, can our heart be somewhat touched by forgiveness and enemy-love.

"Whoever is too quick, and wants to experience things as a purely New Testament person right away, in my judgment, is not a Christian."

Dietrich Bonhoeffer, 5 December 1943
Widerstand und Ergebung, Briefe und Aufzeichnungen aus der Haft (author's translation)

Table of Contents

1

INTRODUCTION

Brevard Childs once wrote that an adequate interpretation of the biblical text "depends on taking the canonical shape with great seriousness."[1] That counsel certainly holds for the Bible book that is popularly known as The Song of Songs, because "Song of songs" – as in "Lord of lords" (Deuteronomy 10:17) – is the Hebraic way of naming the superlative, The *Best* Song, or "The Greatest Song."[2] So, the "(Greatest) Song of (all) songs" is given in the biblical canon as *one unified song* made up of several different voices who speak to one another.

The Greatest Song as a Unified Whole

There is a long history of theologians who have treated the book as an anthology of loose love songs. To be sure, early Jewish interpreters read the songs as a history of Yahweh's love for Israel shown during their journey from the exodus to the Promised Land. Later church fathers like Origen and Jerome set the allegorical pattern for understanding this book as a dialogue between the love of Christ and the church or the redeemed soul. Such a reading was confirmed by the notes added to the Authorized King James translation, so that this allegorical interpretation seemed to become practically canonic for evangelical believers. Although today the practice of interpreting the "two breasts" in The Greatest Song to mean "the Old and the New Testaments" (Hippolytus on 4:5) seems rather far-fetched, yet the problem remains: how can such erotic talk in the greatest song about love fit into the Bible?

When I took a summer fifty years ago to begin translating this book of the Bible from the Hebrew into English, I detected, I thought, a cohesive literary framework to the book, with opposing voices contesting the nature of human sexual desire. I thought I was the first to discover this. Later, after research, I found out that there was a scholarly tradition of reading the book with what was called "the shepherd hypothesis," noting a shepherd in the mix as a third voice along with the Shulammite maiden and Solomon voice.[3]

Many commentators dismiss this three-person interpretation as "the dramatic theory," since the Israelites did not practice drama. But to recognize the book as a chorus of interacting voices is not to call it a "drama." Rejection of this chorus of voices format is often bolstered, I think, by a positivistic hermeneutic that demands word for word clarity, atomistic verse for verse equivalence, but has little sense of narrative continuity.[4]

My careful translation of The Greatest Song[5] assumes an intra-biblical connection – the historical setting of Solomon, who is mentioned in the book – and takes its imaginative literary composition very seriously. The fact that my conception of the book as a chorus of voices has been presented for forty years all over the world, showing the integral unity of the book, is a witness to scholars and ordinary people who read this book as simply a collection of erotic fragments, forcedly allegorized or kept nakedly sexual.

The Bible translations and paraphrases of Bible text used in this book are my responsibility. The best standard Bible translation you can consult for parallel checking might be the New International Version, which distinguishes speakers of different lines as "Lover," "Beloved," and "Friends," somewhat as the an-

cient Greek translation of the Older Testament – the Septuagint
– already did.[6]

Overview

There is a refrain in The Greatest Song spoken by a woman's
voice to "the daughters of Jerusalem" (2:7; 3:5; 8:4). That refrain
—"Do not arouse love until—" not only formulates a key theme
of the whole book, but also helps mark off different episodes in
the narrative about the abduction of a young country woman to
the precincts of Solomon's harem (as happened historically, for
example, in 1 Kings 1:1–4).

The book begins in the setting of the royal bedrooms (1:4),
where a back-and-forth dispute occurs between the country
woman voice and the daughters of Jerusalem. Then comes a dialogue between an admiring courtier and the beautiful abducted
country woman who yearns to be with her country lover (1:2–
2:7).

In a second section (2:8–3:5), the Shulammite country
woman, as she is called (6:13), listens to her lover serenading
her with a love song, while searching for her. The Shulammite
recounts a dream of trying to find her lover.

Then (3:6–4:7) King Solomon, with a large bodyguard and
horses, arrives on the scene in pompous splendor, and makes a
flattering, lewd speech describing to her directly the charms of
her body. In contrast there follows (4:8–5:1) a respectful, yearning song by the country lover searching for his "bride-to-be,"
comparing her to a well-kept, fragrant garden and a protected
spring of sparkling water.

The Shulammite woman responds to both speeches by telling a marriage-night dream that ends fearfully (5:2–8), followed
by an exuberant description of her statuesque lover in absentia
(5:9–6:3).

A climactic confrontation of voices takes place (6:4–13): the King Solomon voice begins to repeat his earlier speech praising the Shulammite's body again, but is interrupted by the shepherd; the Shulammite details her abduction to the king's harem (6:11–12); the daughters of Jerusalem exclaim surprise and jeer at the Shulammite who defends herself.

Then (7:1–8:4) Solomon begins again lustfully to catalog the young woman's charms, until she cuts off the king's speech (7:9b), and pleads with her lover, to whom she belongs, to take her away to the vineyards where their love can be consummated.

Returning to her home territory (8:5–14), the Shulammite woman, reunited with her country lover, together reflect on her chastity, and criticize old King Solomon for his degrading misuse of women, while they anticipate fulfilling their vows of a human bodily love as passionate and as jealous as Yahweh's own love.

The Gospel as the Center of the Greatest Song of Love

The good news of this biblical book is that our God-given sexual desire to be joined as man and woman is very good, a precious human feature in which we may happily exult. The emotional physical union of human lovers is blessed with pleasure and joy when the exciting attraction is disciplined by a jealous commitment to be true to one another. The Greatest Song celebrates the bodily love that unites a woman and a man as a great gift from God.

Even in the beginning, as God was taking time to set up creation, the LORD God discovered, "It is not good that man should be alone. I will make him a helpmeet as his partner" (Genesis 2:18). So as a climax to creation, God created woman. Adam greeted her with a poem:

At last!
Bone of my bone,
flesh of my flesh!
She shall be called "Wo-man,"
for she was "Won-from man." (Genesis 2:23)

For this reason, says Scripture, "A grown man shall leave his father and mother, and cleave to his wife, and they shall become one flesh" (Genesis 2:24). The concluding postscript is also important: "The man and his wife were both naked, and they knew no shame" (Genesis 2:25).

This Genesis charter for joyful, naked, sexual union – to offset human loneliness – is a special blessing of God's grace, but it is also a human feature fraught with trouble. There is something complete about two persons becoming one flesh, one joined physical body – the giving of oneself wholly to the other. You seem to lose yourself in order to find yourself . . . enhanced, completed. And there is something jealous and exclusive about such a willed union. Physical sexuality goes to the roots of personal corporeality; to share it promiscuously tends to destroy a person's self-identity.

Even in the patriarchal, polygamous society of ancient Israel, the rabbis who wrote the biblical Proverbs under the leading of the Holy Spirit picked up the stern word from Mount Sinai about adultery (Deuteronomy 5:18, 21) and gave it a broader, more positive spin:

"A lissome hind, a graceful antelope –
let the breasts of your wife continually intoxicate you;
get carried away, go ahead! again and again in her charms.
But why, my good fellow, do you get carried away by a
    'strange' woman?
Why embrace the bosom of a woman who does not belong
    to you?

– 5 –

The deeds of a man are focused in the eyes of the LORD
    God;
every one of a person's acts the LORD puzzles out:
his own lawlessness will trap the godless living man;
he gets choked by the rope of his own sin."

(Proverbs 5:19–22)

The committed, voluntary, and physical sexual union of a woman and a man goes so deep that great trauma occurs if such a union is forced, uncommitted, or broken (see Matthew 19:3–12). The Greatest Song imaginatively and artistically explores this erotic reality, championed by Genesis and disciplined by Proverbs' wisdom. This Bible book presents the creational grounds for the normative mutuality of the relationship between woman and man that is later confirmed by the Newer Testament (see Ephesians 5:21). The Greatest Song is also unique in that the woman's voice is prominent throughout. Even more than the books of Ruth and Esther, The Greatest Song highlights from a feminine perspective God's good news, blessings, and injunctions.

Reflection

- Everyone reads the Bible from their own perspective. That is one reason why there are so many different interpretations of the Bible. What influences your opinion?

- Do you have difficulty in viewing human sexuality as a good gift from God? If so, why?

SUGGESTED READING: Genesis 2, Proverbs 5, 1 Kings 1–11

2

HISTORICAL BACKGROUND

To understand this book, we must realize the text is a chorus of different voices (like the book of Job) and notice that there is criticism of King Solomon. In the final chapter 8 a voice says:

> Solomon has a vineyard near Baal-hamon, and has placed
> others in charge to watch it . . .
> for its fruits men must pay a 1000 pieces of silver!
> The thousand are yours, (King) Solomon! and may the
> watchmen have hundreds!
> My (single) vineyard here before me is for me alone. (8:11–12)

King Solomon, at the height of his political power, had an opulent life style. An army of court officials were conscripted to administer the supplies needed for his magnificent feasts (1 Kings 4:20–28). The Song mentions just one vineyard Solomon had, one in the north of Israel[1] tended by overseers who had to pay good money for its excess produce. When the speaker contrasts "my one very own vineyard" to the 1000 "vineyards" Solomon has, the response is "You can keep them, Solomon" (8:12b). An attentive listener realizes "vineyards" doubles also for "women," the 1000 (700 princess wives and 300 concubines, women harem for which Solomon was renowned [1 Kings 11:13]). "And may your officials have hundreds," says the speaker: "My one vineyard is singly for my passionate caring love alone" (like the lamb in the story the prophet Nathan used to shame David's adulterous grab of Uriah's "vineyard," 2 Samuel 11:1–12:25).

This third-person reference to Solomon in 8:11–12 is helpful for correcting the widespread assumption that God used Solomon to write The Greatest Song. After all, we are told Solomon wrote 1005 songs (1 Kings 4:32); but Solomon did not compose The Greatest Song. The title given to this biblical book is very carefully formulated: "The Greatest Song, which is *of* Solomon," that is, which is about Solomon. The Greatest Song is actually written in *critique* of Solomon.

Young Solomon loved the Lord, says the Bible, even though he had taken a daughter of Pharaoh as a wife to make a friendly political alliance with Egypt and brought her "into the city of David," his father (1 Kings 3:13). Young Solomon went to the "sacred place" of Gibeon to slaughter 1000 animals as sacrifices to honor and to get the attention of God. When God appeared to Solomon that night in a dream and asked, "What do you want?" Solomon gave his famous answer:

> LORD, my God, I don't know as ruler whether I'm coming
>   or going.
> I don't know how to govern this enormous number of people.
> Please help me discern between good and evil,
> so I can lead this country of *your* people in the right way.
> (1 Kings 3:6–9)

God was so happy Solomon had not asked for riches, a long life, or the death of his enemies, that the LORD promised to make Solomon the wisest man of all time. "And if you keep walking in my ways of shalom (peace)," said God, "I will also make you rich and famous, with a long life" (1 Kings 3:16–28). And the Bible reports that Solomon surpassed the wise men and magicians of Egypt in debate, and was a virtual encyclopedia of herbal and animal knowledge (1 Kings 4:29–34).

Solomon also dedicated his time and commercial deals with

the Syrians to build the temple for the LORD, which God had not allowed King David to do. King Solomon drafted 30,000 Israelites to cut cedars in foreign Lebanon and had 150,000 Canaanite workers in Israel conscripted to quarry and dress stones for the temple. Solomon hired a superb Tyrian artisan in metal to make furniture and basins needed for the temple sacrifices; much of the cypress and sweet-smelling cedarwood and the many rooms were overlaid with gold plate (1 Kings 5–6).

After seven years of constructing God's temple in Jerusalem, King Solomon assembled the elders of Israel, heads of tribes, and leaders of the people to a huge festival to dedicate the temple and to bring into its Most Holy Place the ark of the covenant with the stone tablets of God's Ten Commandments that Moses had received. Then King Solomon prayed a wonderful prayer (1 Kings 8:23–53):

O LORD, God of Israel,
You brought us up out of the land of Egypt long ago,
and You have kept your promises to Moses . . .
and now to my father David with this house we have built
    for You,
we know You can't stay cooped up in a cottage in Jerusalem,
because You are the LORD of heaven and earth,
but we pray, O Almighty Father, that
when we people hurt our neighbor,
and turn our face toward your temple and pray to You in
    heaven,
You will forgive us;
when there is no rain and there is no food, and the econo-
    my goes bad
because we have been greedy and selfish,
if we repent and turn our face toward this temple and pray,
we ask, O LORD, please give us the daily bread we need;
and when even a stranger comes into our land on a visit to

hear about your Rule,
and prays to You in front of your house,
please hear his or her lonely prayer, O LORD,
so that all the earth may know that you, O Yahweh our
    LORD,
are the only true God in the world!

King Solomon's prayer in 1 Kings 8 is comparable to Jesus' John 17 "high priestly" prayer for his followers on earth and those in the world who do not yet believe he was the Messiah, the promised liberator from sin. In his temple dedication prayer, Solomon was at the pinnacle of his wise devotion to the Lord God, truly epitomizing a ruler who keeps God's commandments.

Then things took a turn for the worse. Solomon spent thirteen years building his own palace and associated buildings, including a garage for his 1,400 chariots, stables for his 12,000 imported horses, and a special palace for Pharaoh's daughter in Millo *outside* "the city of David," where the ark of the Lord now resided (1 Kings 7:1–12; 9:1, 24; 10:26–29).

King Solomon spent twice as long building his own palaces as he had spent building the Lord's temple. In fact, Solomon bankrupted the nation! After twenty years of pipeline construction boom, inflation was rampant – silver was only the worth of stones (1 Kings 10:27) – and Solomon had to give Hiram, King of Tyre, twelve cities in Galilee as security for the huge debt Israel had with Syria, 120 talents of gold (approximately $150 million USD; 1 Kings 9:10–14).

At that point, God appeared to Solomon again at Gibeon and said:

I heard your good prayer thirteen years ago at the dedication of my house in Jerusalem.
It was a passionate prayer, Solomon, that made me glad to

be the LORD of Israel,
and I felt very close to you, like twenty years ago at Gibeon,
    remember?
Are you coming or going, Solomon?
If you single-mindedly follow my ordinances, I will estab-
    lish your Rule upon the earth,
but if not, Israel will become a disaster area. . . .
Can you hear me, Solomon? (1 Kings 9:3–9)

The Bible does not report any answer Solomon made to this second visit by God at Gibeon. Instead chapters 9 and 10 of 1 Kings go on to detail the fabulous trade Solomon and Hiram's merchant fleet built up with Southern Arabia, all the way down past Ethiopia to Ophir, bringing back millions of dollars' worth of gold.

And 1 Kings 11 reveals that Solomon went bad. "When Solomon was old, his (many godless) wives turned away his heart after other gods" (1 Kings 11:4). King Solomon worshiped Chemosh, the Moabite god of blood, and Moloch, the Ammonite god who demanded human child sacrifices, because Solomon "cleaved" to his multiple Egyptian, Moabite, Ammonite, Edomite, Sidonian, and Hittite harem of women with a passionate love (1 Kings 11:1–2, 5–8).

The terrible, sad ending of Solomon, like that of King Saul whom God's Spirit had left (1 Samuel 15:35b; 16:14; 18:12; 28:6, 15), deserves to be criticized. That is why Jesus criticized the blinding esteem the populace of his day held for Solomon (Matthew 12:42; Luke 11:31). There is a chill hidden in Christ's remark that Solomon in all his glory was not dressed up as well as a simple wildflower of the field (Matthew 6:28–29; Luke 12:27). It is this harem-hardened, profligate, idolatrous old King Solomon that The Greatest Song is about.

However, next to Solomon in The Greatest Song of love is

a young woman named "the Shulammite" (6:13),[2] who is the main protagonist in the book. She exclaims at the beginning of The Song, "The king has brought me into his bedrooms!" (1:3b). She remonstrates with "the daughters of Jerusalem," an honorific designation for Solomon's harem, "Don't stare at me because I am burned brown by the sun. My brothers made me guard the gardens and vineyards, but my own 'vineyard' I have not guarded well" (1:6). "Why should I be a veiled woman in this harem flock of kept sheep!?" (1:7b) Later in The Song, the Shulammite accosts Solomon himself: Look, I had gone down to the orchard to look at the blossoms, to see whether the grapevines were in bud, whether the luscious pomegranates were in bloom, and before I knew it, I was abducted into the royal chariot (6:11–12)!

Before anyone says that such a fantastic kidnapping in this poetic narrative has no place in the Bible, remember the historical setting of Israel's first kings, what an immoral mess David's polygamous royal family was, and what intrigue and lust Solomon had inherited.

King David, simply by royal whim, had Bathsheba brought to his bedroom while her husband Uriah the Hittite was away fighting the Ammonites in David's army. Then David had General Joab arrange, discreetly, to have Uriah killed. Because King David's deceitful action displeased God, the prophet Nathan promised David that "the sword will never depart from your house" and your own wives will be publicly violated because of what you have done in secret (2 Samuel 12:7–14).

And that happened. Bathsheba's child died, to David's great sorrow (2 Samuel 12:15b–23). Later the beautiful virgin, Tamar (sister of Absalom, David's third son, with his wife Maacah), was tricked and raped by Amnon, David's firstborn son with his wife Ahinoam of Jezreel (who had been a wife of Saul [1 Sam 14:50; 25:43]). Two years later Absalom invited Amnon to a brotherly feast and had him killed in revenge for what Amnon had done to his sister, Tamar (2 Samuel 13).

A few years later Absalom deceitfully gained popularity with the people of Israel and led a revolt against his father David, deposing the king and forcing David out of Jerusalem. On the advice of the wise man Ahitophel, Absalom publicly went in to cohabit with David's concubines, whom David had left behind to take care of things in Jerusalem, to show that he, Absalom, was now in charge of the palace and land (2 Samuel 16:20–22; compare 20:3). However, David's mighty warriors under Joab, Abishai, and Ittai the Gittite fought Absalom's forces and killed Absalom with spears and sword (2 Samuel 18:9–15). David once again mourned a death in the family, this time of his beloved son Absalom (2 Samuel 18:33–19:8).

That David had six wives even before he stole and added Bathsheba to his family, as well as concubines, shows a shadow side of "the man after God's own heart" (1 Samuel 13:14; Acts 13:22) and the corrupt sexual culture of Israel's early monarchy. At the beginning of 1 Kings 1:1–4, the biblical record clearly notes what is significant and relevant for understanding The Greatest Song.

> Now King David was grown old, gray with years, and his servants covered him with cloths and coats, but he didn't get warm. So his servants said to him, "Let my lord the King have them find a young virgin who will come serve the king, be his nurse, and sleep near his belly so that my lord the King may get warm." And they looked for a beautiful girl through the whole land of Israel, and they found Abishag, a Shunammite, and they brought her to the king. And the girl was very, very beautiful. And she served the king as his nurse; but the king did not sleep with her.

When David lay dying, handsome Adonijah, David's fourth son with his wife Haggith and next in line for the throne, prepared to become king of Israel with General Joab and the priest Abiathar's support. But the Queen Bathsheba had plans for her son, the much younger brother Solomon, to succeed David. She visited David, says the Bible, while being nursed by Abishag the Shunammite (1 Kings 1:15), and set in motion a plan to short-circuit Adonijah's ambition. With the help of the wise man Nathan, the priest Zadok, and the military captain Benaiah, Bathsheba had Solomon declared King first instead of his elder brother Adonijah.

So David died, and Solomon became the king of Israel. His elder brother Adonijah fell in line, but later Adonijah came to Bathsheba with a request: could he possibly just have Abishag the Shunammite (whom David did not sleep with) as his wife? Bathsheba said she would ask her boy, King Solomon, who now enjoyed enormous power, and made the request. Solomon saw through the ploy, became very angry, and told his mother, "Why not ask that Adonijah become king!?" So King Solomon sent Captain Benaiah summarily to kill Adonijah.

Solomon as King inherited David's wives and harem. If Adonijah got one concubine, Abishag, as wife, then Adonijah would have a claim on the throne. That is precisely why Absalom publicly went in to sleep with David's concubines, whom David had left in Jerusalem when he fled, to legitimate Absalom's claim to be king. Women were treated as property by powerful men in those biblical days. And the more power royalty had, the more women you could appropriate. Even the visiting Queen of Sheba was mightily impressed at what Solomon had become, and exclaimed, "Happy are your wives . . . who continually attend you and hear your wisdom!" (1 Kings 10:8).

But to be one of 700 wives or 300 concubines in a royal

harem manned by castrated eunuchs was a boring life filled with jealousy, tedium, and degradation. It was David's son Solomon's lascivious desire for this surplus of exotic women (which he had the means to procure) that seduced him to worship their gods and led to the break-up of Israel and the dereliction of God's people.

God gave The Greatest Song, as we shall see, as a word of correction to the evil that *old* King Solomon carried on in the later years of his reign, when God's blessings went to his head and he no longer kept covenant with the LORD God, but gave way to his insatiable, lawless desires (1 Kings 11:9–10).

Reflection

- This graph shows the trajectory of Solomon's faith life. Could you graph your own faith life, and tell about its ups and downs?

Solomon's Faith in 1 Kings

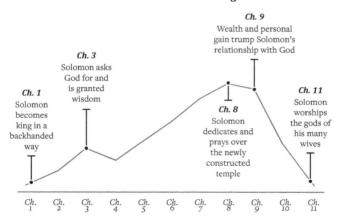

Ch. 9
Wealth and personal gain trump Solomon's relationship with God

Ch. 3
Solomon asks God for and is granted wisdom

Ch. 1
Solomon becomes king in a backhanded way

Ch. 8
Solomon dedicates and prays over the newly constructed temple

Ch. 11
Solomon worships the gods of his many wives

Ch. 1   Ch. 2   Ch. 3   Ch. 4   Ch. 5   Ch. 6   Ch. 7   Ch. 8   Ch. 9   Ch. 10   Ch. 11

SUGGESTED READING: Proverbs 1–3; 7–9; Matthew 5–7:27

3

BIBLICAL WISDOM LITERATURE AND TELLING TRUE STORIES

The Greatest Song is a highly poetic presentation of conflicting voices around the theme of desire, anticipated erotic union, and abiding human love that is jealous and faithful as God ordained. The Song coheres as one narrative piece, like the book of Job. It is an *imaginative* account of a struggle between human love and lust, foolishness and wisdom, and how God sees the nub of our human nature. The Song is not a report of an historical event; it is not an anthology of stray love songs. It is an exemplary account of what did happen in ancient Israel, what has happened in many contexts, what is happening, and what shall continue to happen so long as humans are sinful, redeemable, loving, and hating corporeal creatures.

The Greatest Song as Wisdom Literature

The Greatest Song is an instructive tale of biblical wisdom literature. That is, writing written under the leading of the Holy Spirit by educated counselors, teachers, judges, and scribes who were leaders in ancient Israel during the monarchy (like Nathan, Ahitophel, Hushai, and Hezekiah's cabinet advisors [compare Proverbs 25:1]) and later during and after the exile of Israel and Judah (sage court counselors like Daniel and his friends, Mordecai, Nehemiah, and Ezra). *Young* Solomon, even as king, epitomized such "wise persons," for he wrote 3,000 proverbs (1

Kings 4:32) – clusters of epigrammatic poems, anecdotal tales, and metaphorical conundrums.

A typical feature of biblical wisdom literature is the juxta-position of opposite positions to clarify what choices we face and which – despite appearances – would be truly the right decision. For example, chapter 1 of the book of Proverbs quotes the come-on of a professional gang of house invaders and robbers:

> Come with us! Let's ambush the gullible!
> Let's swallow them alive like hell!
> We'll find all kinds of valuables and fill our houses with
>   booty –
> Join us, we'll split the money evenly . . . (1:11–14)

The next verses counter the lucrative invitation:

> Don't take the bait, my dear fellow.
> Such conspirators are quick to shed blood.
> The traps they set for unsuspecting folk
> snap shut on themselves, finish off themselves! (1:15–19)

And then Solomon's editor, led by the Spirit, concludes the opening chapter with a passionate speech by the voice of Wis-dom herself:

> "You simpletons! Listen to me, Wisdom!
> Let me pour my Spirit[1] out upon you.
> Follow my lead and hear my reproof.
> Choose to stand in awe of the LORD and God's ordinances.
> To be wayward or complacent is to commit suicide!" (1:22–33)

Proverbs 9 portrays the central message of chapters 1–9 by having two women, standing in front of open doors, make al-most identical invitations to the younger generation: the meal of bread and wine is all ready! Come on in, and sup with me. The Woman Wisdom adds, "Don't be immature; walk the Way of insight." And the Woman Foolishness adds, "Stolen water is sweet, and eating intimately together in secret is very pleasurable!" Which woman's invitation is accepted is a matter of life *or* death, says chapter 9 (v. 18). A paragraph in between the two woman's solicitations gives the key point of the confrontation, which wise persons accept and foolish people shrug off: standing in awe of God is the *beginning* of wisdom, and knowing what is holy contributes true insightfulness (9:7–12).

Proverbs 7:6–23 spins a tale of seduction and concludes with a moral application, which is a standard but indirect way for both the judges and the educated scribal teachers in Israel to make the word of the LORD known to people. Such a method is shown in "The fable of the trees," told by Jothan (the youngest son of Gideon), after Abimelech organized a massacre of their seventy brothers by his kinfolk of Shechem in order to push himself forward to become king in Israel (Judges 9:7–21).

This "storytelling" or "guess-the-riddle" way of teaching was used by the judge Samson to outsmart the angry Philistine relatives of his first wife (Judges 14):

Out of the eater came eats.
Out of the stronger came sweets! (v. 17)

Nathan's fictional account of the poor man whose one beloved lamb was snatched away by the rich landowner to feed a guest pinned King David to the wall on his flagrant adulterous sin (2 Samuel 12:1–7). In 1 Kings, young Solomon's charade in judging which of the two prostitutes was the mother of the living baby follows the same "make-believe" pattern – Solomon never intended to cut the baby in half to administer wise justice (1 Kings 3:16–26).

AN OLDER TESTAMENT PARABLE RENDERED VERY DIRECTLY (author's translation of Proverbs 7:6–23)

Once upon a time, as I was standing at the window opening of my house, from behind my shutters I happened to look down (upon the street), and I saw among the inexperienced fellows – I took note of a young fellow among the boys there, who lacked both brains and guts. He was loafing around on the street not far from "her" corner. Finally he started to step off the way to her house. It was in the cool of dusk falling, as the day darkles into evening, around the time (of the new moon) when the night is really darkness.

Did you see it? It happened! The woman accosts him.

She wears the fashion of a professional whore, and cunning stealth shapes her every move. She's brassy and catty. She can't keep her feet still inside her own place. For a while she lurks outside between the houses, then for a while it's right out in the open; she seems to be lying in wait near every street corner – there! She has grabbed hold of the boy. Now she kisses clinging to him. . . .

She puts on a bold face and says to him: "(Hello!) I was owing some sacrifices of shalom. Today I paid up all the outstanding vows; so I'm free to feast! That's why I came out to meet you. I've been so looking forward to meeting you face to face, and now I've found you! I've made my little couch all ready with fine tapestries, made it plush with brilliantly colored linen goods out of Egypt! I've touched up my larger bed with sprinkles of myrrh and aloes and cinnamon spices – Come on, let's get drunk the whole night until morning on some red-hot loving! Let's drown ourselves in passionate caresses! The husband's not home, you know; he went on a long (business) trip, took his moneybags with him; he won't be back home until it's full moon. . . ."

This is the way she twists and turns him around by her very persuasive talk. She seduces him by the utterly lovely, pursed movements of her lips.

There he goes! walking behind her like an ox headed for slaughter, like a dog about to be whipped! The fool doesn't know that his very life is at stake. He's like a little bird flying smack into a trap – he won't know it until (her) jagged arrow splits his liver in half.

So now, children (– parents, do you hear me? Listen closely to what my mouth is saying): Never let your heart be sidetracked into the ways of the Strange Woman. Never get lost in her well-beaten crossroads! because there is a horde of victims she has prostrated; the most mighty men are among all those whom she has extinguished. The house of the Strange Woman opens the ways to hell! (Follow her, my son, my daughter, my parent, and) you end up sunk in the dark, no-exit rooms of Death!

The story told in Proverbs 7:6–23 is not an account of what literally took place, but is a *parable* of what often happens when young men go off on their own and are fooled by their own legitimate desires. Young Solomon was used by God's Spirit to picture this scenario in chapter 7, tell its counsel, and put it in writing for the naive to learn what God wants. Old King Solomon forgot this very word from the LORD, which he had written down when young, and walked into the trap of lawless sexual desires.

Who is Listening?

According to the Bible, God originally seemed to speak quite directly to people. God walked and talked with Adam and Eve (Genesis 3:8–19) and personally questioned and cursed Cain for murdering his brother Abel (Genesis 4:3–16). God told Noah how to prepare for the devastating coming flood (Genesis 6:11–21), called Abram for his sojourn to Canaan, and made far-reaching promises about Abraham's descendants (Genesis 12:1–3). God spoke to Moses from a burning bush (Exodus 3) and often conversed with Moses during the time at Mount Sinai and during the Israelites' desert journey. God still spoke one-on-one to Joshua; God authorized Joshua to order the priests to move the ark of the covenant ahead of the Israelites when they crossed the Jordan into the Promised Land (Joshua 3:7–9).

But after Joshua's death, a new generation grew up ignorant of the LORD and God's great deeds for the nation of Israel (Judges 2:6–10). The covenanted people of God did what was right in their own eyes (Judges 17:6) rather than follow the ordinances spelled out by the LORD. God did raise up judges filled by the Spirit (Judges 2:16; 3:10) to try to lead God's people. Their new homeland was still filled with Canaanite tribes practicing fertility religions (e.g., the worship of power-hungry Baal and Ashtoroth, promoting sexual promiscuity). However, the judges themselves were inconstant; so that by the time Samuel was apprenticed to the incompetent priest Eli, Scripture says, "The word of the LORD was rare in those days" (1 Samuel 3:1). God did not talk much in those days, since hardly anybody was listening!

There were those whose roles should have or did require communicating with God, directly or indirectly:

- *Priests* had served God's people since Aaron was ordained by God in the wilderness, doing the bloody work of sacrifices for God's forgiveness of repentant sinners.
- By the time of Elijah and Elisha (compare 2 Kings 2:3), *prophets* had gradually come to be trained in schools. The prophets' specified task was "to sound out the word of the LORD" (1 Samuel 9:27). They usually made known what God told them to say by preaching, "Thus says the LORD!" (compare Amos 1:3, 6, 9, 11, 13).
- *Kings* followed the judges in Israel around 1100

BC and were called by God and anointed to administer justice and to lead God's people in war (compare 1 Samuel 8).

Next to priests, prophets, and kings – who were mouthpieces for God on earth to lead God's listening people – were the wise men and women in Israel. "The wise" were those who could read and write; the scribes who kept records in writing, counseled rulers, and taught the people with stories and songs. They were the literati who knew the LORD's *torah* (God's commandments) well and could relate spirited principles to specific matters of human judgment. There are many examples of wise men and women in the Older Testament:

- Joseph, through God-given wisdom, became the Hyksos Pharaoh of Egypt's Prime Minister because Joseph could interpret dreams and both form and administer policies that were fruitful (Genesis 41:38–40).[2]
- Balaam, son of Beor of Pethor (on the Euphrates river), was a renowned wise man. He was consulted by the Moabite King Balak when the Moabite nation didn't know what to do about the horde of Israelites camped on their borders, headed for Canaan (Micah 6:5).
- Absalom pretended to be a wise man to cultivate popular approval (1 Samuel 15:1–6).

There were "wise counselors" among other Israelite leaders, too, such as the seventy "elders" the Holy Spirit qualified to assist Moses in ruling the wandering tribes of Israel (Numbers 11:16–30). Later, they were accustomed to sit at the gates of their towns to offer just judgments for the citizens on their disputes (Deuteronomy 21:18–21).

That the wise had a discernible task among God's people is subtly disclosed near the end of King Saul's career. Saul went to visit a witch in Endor because the LORD did not answer Saul anymore, neither through the Urim and Thumim (dice the priests used for very grave decisions, compare Leviticus 8:18), the prophets, nor by dreams (1 Samuel 28:6).[3] We know that when King David's wise man, Ahitophel, spoke it "was as if one consulted the oracle of God" (2 Samuel 6:23). Yet God used the wise man Hushai to confuse the advice Ahitophel gave to renegade Absalom (2 Samuel 17:14).

The Bible notes that there were wise women too, such as the judge Deborah, whom God sent to give Barak a little backbone to fight the Canaanite oppressors (Judges 4). Then Deborah composed the great, history-laden song of Judges 5.

In another example, Joab commissioned a wise woman of Tekoa (the prophet Amos' hometown) to put on a dramatic act for King David. She acted as if she were about to lose her banished son, so that when King David judged the case positively he would reconcile himself with his banished son Absalom (2 Samuel 14:1–24).

A wise woman saved the city of Abel, her home, from destruction when she debated over the wall with General Joab. Rather than have the whole city razed, she convinced her townspeople to behead the Benjaminite insurrectionist Sheba, son of Bichri, who had taken refuge in Abel (2 Samuel 20:1–22). It's clear wise women as well as wise men played a leadership role among the illiterate people of God as well as at the educated court.

The Importance of Wise Men and Women

Even King Solomon, who epitomized the pith of "the wise," had counselors near his throne. Scripture mentions that the reformer king Hezekiah's "wise officials" edited several chapters of Solomon's proverbs (Proverbs 25:1), with the intent to help provide good, reforming directions for the governors of the people outside the chief city of Jerusalem.

There is evidence that wise men and women had a different status from priests and prophets in Israel. This was made clear by the enemies of the prophet Jeremiah when they said, "Let's get him because *torah* instruction by priests, *counsel* by the wise, and *the word* (of the LORD) by the prophets are not going to disappear" (Jeremiah 18:18).

The Babylonian king Nebuchadnezzar's deportation policy made certain that Judah King Jehoiakim's wise men, like Daniel, Hananiah, Mishael, and Azariah, were not made to dig ditches in Babylon but were incorporated as counselors into his corps of Chaldean sorcerers and astrologers (Daniel 1:1–4, 17–20). It is significant that still later – after Cyrus' edict let the Jews return to the Promised Land to rebuild a temple and the wall around Jerusalem, in the absence of Davidian kings and post-Malachi prophets – a Jewish eunuch like Nehemiah and a scribe like Ezra came to the fore to set policies for the returned exiles.

Qohelet (the main speaker in the book of Ecclesiastes) also served in the traditional position of "Teacher" (or Jewish Counselor, a reflective and wise dispenser of God's will for righteous living), an office carried on by the writers of the Apocrypha and leadership that devolved into the Sadducean scribes and Pharisees of Christ's day on earth.

Jesus as the Ultimate Wise Man

Jesus as rabbi (John 11:8, 28; 20:16) exemplifies the role of "the wise." He crystallizes the wise way of making God's will known to people, scattered like sheep in God's world, and to their would-be leaders: parable stories and posing enigmatic contrasts through the "Yes, but . . ." formula to demonstrate alternative decisions.

Matthew 5–7 illustrates clearly the method of the wise.[4] The beatitudes (Matthew 5:3–11) are Newer Testament proverbs – terse, enigmatic theses that startle the hearers into slowly discovering the compressed meaning. In these teachings, Jesus employed the provocative method of juxtaposing older, fixed regulations and newer, outrageous formulas:

> "You have heard it was said, 'You shall not commit adultery.'
> *But* ... you commit adultery just by looking at a woman with lust. So gouge out your eyes!" (5:27–30)
> "You have heard it was said, 'You shall love your neighbor and hate your enemy,'
> *but* I say, Love your enemies, and pray for those who persecute you.
> Wise up! Become like your heavenly Father – completely good!" (5:43–48)

Jesus' favorite way of giving redemptive direction was to make up imaginative stories (as did Jothan, Nathan, the wise woman of Tekoa, and King Solomon in Proverbs 7), such as the seven parables collected in Matthew 13. Jesus' disciples were mystified at these public storytelling events, and asked, "Why do you speak to the people in parables?" And Jesus' oblique answer was, "I teach in parables so that hearers take the time to become listeners with open hearts inquisitive for good news, rather than remain blasé 'show me' persons who want to be spoon-fed instructions with miracle entertainment on how to get ahead" (compare Matthew 13:10–17; Mark 4:10–12). Then Jesus explained the parable of the sower and the different soils and the parable of the weeds infesting the field of wheat to help his chosen disciples start to grasp that following in his footsteps would be arduous, fruitful, conflicted, and ultimately blessed (Matthew 13:18–23, 36–43).

BEATITUDE WISDOM BIBLE SONG

1. Blest are the con - trite hearts: God's king - dom
2. Blest are the gen - tle meek: they shall re -
3. Blest are the mer - ci - ful: mer - cy they
4. Blest, those who rec - on - cile: chil - dren of
5. Blest, you who suf - fer harm when it is

comes for them. Blest are the wronged and
ceive the earth. Blest are those hun - gry
shall re - ceive. Blest are the ones whose
God are they. Blest are those hurt for
for Christ's sake. Bear with the per - se -

griev - ing ones: they shall be com - fort - ed.
for the right: they shall be sat - is - fied.
hearts are pure: they sure - ly shall see God.
Je - sus' sake: God's rule shall make them whole.
cut - ing ones: God shall give you great joy.

6 Act like the salt of earth:
   salt without taste is waste.
   Shine like a lighthouse in the night;
   hide not your lamp of love.

7 Point to our covenant Lord
   with every word and deed;
   then all may see the works you do
   and praise the Lord our God.

Text: Matthew 5:3–16; vers. Calvin Seerveld, 1984, ©
Tune: J. Chetham's A Book of Psalmody, 1718; harm. Samuel S. Wesley, 1872

SM
WIRKSWORTH

The key point here is that instead of using the prophets' direct manner (e.g., "Thus says the Lord!"), Jesus would ask a question to engage the inquirers (compare Mark 8:27–30). Jesus did not serve as traditional Israelite priest who sacrificed animals in the temple, but came to be the sacrificial lamb itself (John 1:29, 36).

Jesus modeled the age-old pedagogical method of the wise counselors in history: elicit surprise with an imaginative, poetically formulated story (compare Luke 18:98–14); instruct with "Yes, *but . . .*" indirection in order to engage the listener, and try to take them a step further.

This wise way of making God's word known was normally roundabout, using question-and-answer as puzzles to lead to a vivid nugget of true insight that should be taken to heart and played with to tease out its implications. Students always need to complicate what their good teachers have simplified for them, so that the students can truly own the knowledge themselves rather than parrot back what they are told.

Jesus' Rabbinic Method of Instruction (author's translation of Luke 11:14–28)

There was Jesus busy exorcizing an evil spirit – it was one that made you deaf and dumb. When the evil spirit was expelled, the dumb person spoke, and the crowd was dumbfounded. But some of them said, "He's exorcizing demons by Beelzebul, the ruler of demons!" Others beseeched Jesus for a (special) sign from heaven – that was their way of tempting him.

Jesus, however, fathomed their innermost thoughts, and told them, "Every ruling kingdom divided against itself will go to pieces; household upon household will topple. So if the Satan is divided against Satan self, how can Satan's ruling kingdom stay standing? [I say that] because you say that I exorcize demons by Beelzebul. If then I cast out evil spirits by Beelzebul, in whose [power] do your disciples[5] exorcize! Do you want your own exorcizing disciples then to be your condemning judges? **But** if I am exorcizing the evil spirits by God's finger [the Holy Spirit[6]], then the Ruling kingdom of God has unexpectedly come upon you!

"When the strongman [Satan] armed to the teeth guards his very own expensive house, his belongings are safe. But when someone still stronger [Jesus Christ] comes along, that one will conquer the strongman, take away all his armaments in which he trusted, and divvy up his possessions as spoils.

"Whoever does not belong to me is against me, and whoever doesn't pull together with me, dissipates [my strength].

"When the befouling spirit has gone out of a man, it wanders through wastelands looking for refreshment, and when it hasn't found any resting place, that dirty spirit says, 'I'm gonna go back to my [old] house where I came from.' And coming back, it finds the [old] man swept clean and tidied up [but empty]. So then that dirty evil spirit goes out and gets seven other spirits more tricky than himself, and going into the fellow they settle down there [permanently].[7] The last days of that person, I tell you, become worse than the earlier ones."[8]

Now it happened that while Jesus was speaking these words, some woman or other in the crowd raised her voice and hollered to him, "Blessed is the belly that carried you around, and the tits that gave you suck!"[9]

But Jesus said, "That's fine [lady], **but** the point is: *Blessed are those who hear the word of God, and are busy doing it!*"[10]

This special, imaginative way of the wise (and Jesus) can make God's will known to people with the Holy Spirit's authority (Matthew 7:28–29). This approach to God's revelation is the exact way God's word is given to us – as literature. Hearing God speak through written revelation is more than a matter of lingual-analytic intelligence. Hearing God speak demands an accepting, repentant heart that can take in the literarily written work with adult responsibility but a listening, childlike imagination.

The Greatest Song of the Older Testament is the Holy Spirit-breathed writing of such wise scribes. Prime candidates for the scribes God used to write down The Greatest Song are the counselors of old King Solomon's court, whom his son Rehoboam inherited when he succeeded Solomon.

When Solomon's son Rehoboam asked the wise in his cabinet how he should rule God's people, those older counselors – who had experienced Canaanite slave labor and orgies under old King Solomon, reported in 1 Kings 11 – advised the new king to lighten the yoke of governance and to show a willingness to serve the people rather than to lord it over them. But Rehoboam rejected their sage advice and followed the counsel of his younger wise officials – who had grown up with Rehoboam's privileged youth – to be even harsher than his father Solomon had been. As a result – in line with God's plan to punish Solomon for his profligacy – ten tribes of Israel broke away from Rehoboam and followed Jeroboam Nebatson as king (1 Kings 11:26–12:29).

It would have been normal for the aged, rejected counselors of Rehoboam to leave Jerusalem and join the kingdom under Jeroboam. A hint that this might have happened is found in The Greatest Song, when the beauty of the Shulammite maiden is compared to Tirzah and Jerusalem.

> You are as pleasantly clad as Tirzah,
> as beautiful as Jerusalem. (6:4)

The best time to compare pleasing Tirzah with the incomparable Jerusalem would have been when Tirzah was the capital city of the ten tribes of Israel, from around 920 BC until Omri became sole king of Northern Israel. Omri later built up Samaria as a new capital of Israel, around 875 BC. (1 Kings 14:17; 15:21, 33; 16:6, 8–9, 15–28).[11]

In the whole chorus of different voices that constitute the text of the Greatest Song, mentioning Tirzah fits very well with the idea that God used the old licentious Solomon's former intimate counselors, who fled to give counsel to the kings in rebellious Tirzah, to compose a poetic account that pulls God's good news about human erotic love out of the black hat of old King Solomon's debauchery.

Reflection

- What are the main differences of the distinct office of "wise counselor" in the Bible next to the special calling and task of prophet, priest, and king?

- Did you, like Jesus' closest disciples, wonder why Jesus told parables to people (Matthew 13:10)? Do you understand Jesus' answer?

- If you see the similarity of Jesus saying, "Gouge out your eyes" (Matthew 5:29) and young Solomon's saying "Cut the baby in half" (I Kings 3:28), does it help you understand how to read the wisdom of the Bible? (The church father Origen read Matthew 19:10–12, and possibly castrated himself!)

SUGGESTED READING: The Greatest Song 1–8

CONTRASTING TENOR OF OPPOSING VOICES ON LOVE

The Shulammite's Brothers

The Song opens with the Shulammite country maiden exclaiming, "The king has brought me into his bedrooms! [1:3b] Why should I be a veiled woman in this herd of your bedfellows? [1:7b]. My brothers were infuriated with me, and made me guard the vineyards all alone – my own vineyard I have left unguarded" (1:6b).

The Shulammite's brothers are mentioned at the beginning of The Song (as "the sons of my mother," which hints at disapproval) as being instrumental in her present danger, since she was abducted to the royal harem (6:11–12). At the closing of The Song (8:8–9), the brothers are mentioned again as having been concerned about the virginity of their little sister.

> "What shall we do for our sister when she develops breasts
> and the potential lovers begin to crowd around?
> If she is an open door, we'll barricade the way to her with
> planks of wood;
> if she remains chaste, we will give her a silver crown."

In response to her brothers, the Shulammite can say, "I came through the ordeal like a wall, and my breasts are fully round, large, and mature. Give me your blessing now of shalom" (8:10).

The two mentions of the brothers at the beginning and at

the end act like bookends to the story of the Shulammite's being taken captive, away from her country home, and brought to the city harem of King Solomon to become another concubine. The narrative is an imaginative replay, as it were, of what happened in 1 Kings 1:1–4 – *from the girl's point of view!*

The Daughters of Jerusalem

The beginning of The Song quotes the tired compliments (1:2–3) the daughters of Jerusalem were taught to practice to make themselves attractive to the king. The harem women take turns jousting with this new lovely virgin and competitor for Solomon's affection who was picked up by the king's servants. "If you don't want to be here," says a head harem woman, "Well, get out! and follow the shepherds! Go feed your goats around the huts of the shepherds" (1:8).

In chapter 3, the commotion caused among the daughters of Jerusalem by Solomon's arrival with pomp and circumstance to impress his newest prospective concubine subtly indicates how boring harem life is for a woman. As one in a thousand you spend most of your life waiting, captive and secluded in a pampered nest of bickering and jealousy. For Solomon to show up with his stretch Cadillac, surrounded by an impressive honor guard of sixty armed soldiers (3:6–11) is enough to palpitate any harem woman's heart.

But the Shulammite is not swayed from remembering her true lover back home and repeats her remonstration to the harem: "Don't try to make me give myself bodily in 'love' to somebody who only wants me for sexual pleasure" (2:7, 3:5). "Can't you harem women understand that?" (5:8). The captive harem women cannot understand her commitment to a country shepherd next to the prospect of being with a King and possibly giving birth to a boy "in the line of David."[1] "Why do you keep on so forcefully appealing to us to stop encouraging you to yield your body to the entreating King?" Only after the Shulammite extols the appearance of her absent lover at length (5:10–16), do the harem women soften up, to say, "Can we help you find your true love?" (6:1)

King Solomon and the Shulammite's Lover

When the country lover shows up for the imagined confrontation with King Solomon, he startles and impresses the harem women (6:10). The daughters of Jerusalem revert to their quarrelsome siding with the lascivious king. "Turn around! turn around, oh Shulammite! Turn around, turn around," they jeer at her confused desperation, "so we can see you!" (6:13). The harem then fades away as audience for and participant in the Shulammite's would-be seduction by King Solomon.

The missing shepherd lover is vitally present in the Shulammite's consciousness during the whole narrative; she refers to him constantly from the very start of her struggle (1:3a, 7). The Song introduces her lover as a bounding young deer or gazelle, singing to her about the lovely springtime in the country with the wildflowers appearing and the fig tree and vineyards beginning to bud and blossom with fruit and fragrant smells. He sings about a time for lovers to go for a walk together in the fields and apple orchards, enjoying each other's closeness outdoors (2:8–14). The tone of the shepherd lover's appeal is pleasant and respectful; he waits to see her face and hear her melodious voice.

In contrast, Solomon's speech to the Shulammite is blunt. He accosts her with contrived compliments, as if gauging her like a piece of flesh. Solomon tries to affect a pastoral idiom he has no knowledge of to insinuate himself into her world, but the attempt yields outlandish, bizarre comparisons (4:1–5):

> Your hair is like a herd of goats wending its way down
> Mount Gilead . . .

> Your teeth are like a flock of sheep newly shorn coming up
>   out of their watering place . . .
> not one of which is barren, all of which soon will be bearing
>   twins . . .
> (hint, hint, you could be bearing twins in the royal line of
>   David, woman!)

Even when Solomon uses a metaphor closer to his court-bred life, the comparison is heavy-handed, overblown:

> Your neck is like a tower of David built for battle, on which
> 1000 shields might be hung! (4:4)

Solomon's frontal analysis of the Shulammite's physical attributes is a rough, macho reflection of what *he* desires. Compare the country lover's discrete description of "my sister, my bride-to-be," whom he envisions captive somewhere high up on Mount Shenir or Hermon in a den of carnivorous lions or the caves of dangerous leopards (4:8). The country lover reports how the Shulammite's *love* has affected him:

> The glance of your eyes, a movement of your throat, the
>   odor of your oils,
> the words from your lips, the smell of your clothes, transfix
>   me with a sweet happiness,
> he says, "as if honey and milk lay under your tongue." You,
> "my sister, my bride-to-be," are like a garden of exquisite,
> exotic spices – nard and saffron, calamus and cinnamon,
> frankincense, myrrh, and aloe! like a spring of bubbling waters flowing down from Mount Lebanon (4:9–15). But you
> are an enclosed garden, a well covered over, a lovely fountain sealed tight – not promiscuously open to all comers
> (4:12).

The shepherd lover does not emphasize the Shulammite's naked body parts, but depicts the aura of her enchanting presence, telling of intimacy while keeping a decorum of distance.

When Solomon continues his pitch for the Shulammite's affection, he doggedly repeats his artificial phrases as if he has rehearsed his speechwriter's text:

> "Your hair is like a herd of goats wending its way down Mount Gilead . . .
> Your teeth are like a flock of mother sheep newly shorn coming up out of their watering place – all soon to be bearing twins, not one barren." (6:5b–7)

The repeated phrases are such a deft literary touch. They are a cunning way to show Solomon's insincerity, the practiced technique of an experienced seducer.

When that fails, Solomon is depicted as throwing caution to the winds and revealing his lust for the virgin maiden. Solomon now (7:1–9a) describes her intimate areas – "the curve of your thighs . . . your navel is like a little round cup and needs to be filled full with spicy wine . . . your belly is like a shimmering mound of wheat . . . your two breasts . . . your neck . . . your eyes . . . your nose . . . your head . . . your flowing locks of hair . . . ."

> "How well formed, how pleasantly formed you are . . . compared to the most delightfully enchanting things.
> Your flowing figure reminds me of a palm tree, your breasts are like clusters of dates – I said to myself, I will go climb the palm tree! I will go grab hold of its date clusters!
> Your breasts will roll over me like clusters of grapes!
> The breath of your nose will fill me like the smell of ripe apples!
> Your kisses will flow like sweet wine! –"

This is the speech of a lecher out of control, with the telltale sign of a pornographic mentality, which dissociates a person into body parts. Solomon's chapter 7 verbal assault upon the Shulammite woman is a raping speech, which she cuts off witheringly in mid-verse, as it were: "The wine of my kisses shall flow straight to the mouth of only my lover, not touching at all such well-worn lips" (7:9bc).

Careful reading catches the radical difference in the two male voices addressing the Shulammite: the cheerful, homely allusions to her matching and illuminating the fertile fragrant herbs and flowers of the field versus the forced, practiced, contrived, and exaggerated fixation on her body parts. The opposition is comparable to the honest, forthright, and vulnerable confession of Job versus the carefully honed pomposities of Job's friends. The shepherd lover's words have the tenor of wholesome, intimate, respectful love versus late King Solomon's lascivious, indulgent lust to have in his grasp more and more deflowered women.

Contrasting Voices

The principal protagonists in The Song are the Shulammite maiden with her true shepherd lover. They are beset by Solomon – the powerful, authoritarian, anointed King of the LORD turned into the dissolute profligate of 1 Kings 11. We may assume God's Spirit used the skilled elderly counselors rejected by Rehoboam (who knew about late King Solomon's orgies, see p. 30) to write The Greatest Song since the piece has a vivid, knowledgeable feel and slips in the place name of Tirzah (6:4), in Northern Israel, where the writers of this book may have been located.[2]

Solomon's first comment to the Shulammite reveals how godless the Solomon represented in The Song has become: "You remind me of my warhorse in the chariot of Pharaoh, my lovely one" (1:9). Solomon is complimenting the Shulammite on her fiery, free-spirited character and refreshing protestations compared to the docile, used "thistles" of his harem (2:2). But the writers God used to inscribe this book are damning Solomon by his own mouth; Israel's kings were forbidden by God to possess warhorses or to make an alliance with Egypt (Deuteronomy 17:14–17). King Solomon's first utterance of flattery is already presented as judged and self-serving.

While Solomon bombards the country girl with promises of jewelry and gold ornaments and boasts about his palace rooms crafted with sweet-smelling cedar and imported Phoenician juniper wood, the Shulammite, tanned by working outside in the hot sun (1:6), claims only to be a simple wildflower from the Sharon plains. She is content to lie in the grass or sheltered by grape arbor shade with her shepherd lover, dallying with caresses (1:10–2:4). The opposition is not so much country versus city culture or even natural simplicity versus luxury, as it is the difference between wholesome, voluntary mutual dalliance of a young couple next to an older paramour trying to buy affection with presents.

The Song is *not* contrasting prim (e.g., Victorian Christian) etiquette against honest-to-goodness human passion. God's word here is delighting in the whole-bodied joy of the faithfully committed young Shulammite woman and her shepherd lover, while exposing the degrading meanness of a physically aggrandizing, dominant man.

> "My lover's head lay between my breasts like a little pouch of myrrh." (1:13)
> "He would lead me out to a hidden grape arbor, and cover me there with his love!" (2:4)

Such a confession by the Shulammite maiden bespeaks passion with an unaffected innocence. Their invitations to one another to enjoy each other's bodily gardens dances with promise, anticipation, trust, and a fulfilling sensuous peace, free of compulsion.

> "Yes, let my beloved come to his garden, and enjoy its sweet fruits."
> "I'll come to my garden, my sister, my bride-to-be, to gath-

er my myrrh and spice, to savor the honey of my honeycomb, and drink deep of the wine and the milk."
(4:16–5:1)

The privacy of such erotic activity and the will to have its
mutually joyful action sanctioned by her mother and brothers
(8:1–2) does not cramp their love, but frees it from guilt.

Such frolicsome erotic abandon —

"Arise, beloved, my beautiful one, come wander away with
me . . ." (2:10b–14)
"Oh, yes, do come to gather in the red lilies" – (6:2)

is outside the Solomon figure's purview. Solomon knows and
wants single-mindedly the sexual pleasure of multiple breasts
rolling over him, his climbing up women like palm trees to
pluck their dates, being engulfed by perfumed kisses and the soft
flesh of tongue and palette (7:7–9a). For Solomon the black-out
ecstasy of physical orgasm is the epitome of "love." You as man
satisfy yourself and conquer the woman.

Reflection

- Did you mark the Shulammite's praise of her lover's
  appearance is in the third person (5:10–16), while he
  is absent? Do you catch the difference from Solomon's
  frontal description of the Shulammite in the second
  person (7:1–9a), to her face?

- Did you detect the false, aggressive note in Solomon's
  speeches about his passion for the Shulammite maiden?

SUGGESTED READING: Reread The Greatest Song, marking
who is saying which lines, so you catch a sense of the chorus of
voices.

5

A GODLY NUGGET OF WISDOM

The Shulammite maiden's disagreement with her overprotective brothers; her combative interaction with the daughters of Jerusalem harem; the utterly different tones of the shepherd's expressions of desire and Solomon's possessive, commanding insinuations; the outright disconnect between the Shulammite's life experience and Solomon's lifelong royal prerogative to get what he wants (1:9–11, 12–14; 6:5a): all these oppositions and juxtapositions set up the very tension to be expected in biblical wisdom literature. Good and evil are both represented in force. Their dissembled conflict needs to be discerned and judged so that we, by attending to the opposing stances, may become wise. The refrain in The Song sums up the point of this chorus of biblical wisdom:

"Daughters of Jerusalem! I plead with you –
do you not know the gazelles and the hinds of the plain
    country?
I plead with you,
Never try to arouse or excite a beloved till the love come
    naturally." (2:7; 3:5; 5:5; 8:4)

In effect, this refrain is saying: Don't you captive, exploited women, slave to a king's cravings, want to know the unhindered freedom of young deer to frolic in the countryside? Never try to stimulate passion artificially! Never hurry the path of love and force its power, but let the attraction between a woman and a man grow naturally, slowly flowering within the bond of building trust and commitment, till it is ready to be joyfully experienced as shalom (peace) – a surprising blessing! Let time turn quirks and blemishes into badges of sweet, shared intimacy rather than obstacles to respect. Let the excitement of full bodily union, where two persons become joined as *one flesh*, be a discovery of pleasure and joy that comes upon you as a gift!

The refrain honors the reality that genuine passionate human love does not take place somewhere in an airtight compartment of untrammeled delight or on a remote Romantic island where impurity does not exist. Genuine love happens in the context of competing interests, power dynamics, and seductive blandishments that buffet, test, and would sully chaste passion. Late King Solomon, with his overblown harem of exotic women, is a good Older Testament foil for normative erotic love. The fact that the refrain is formulated as a negative injunction to the harem and any naive listeners should not fool anybody. It is an informed, wise, and positive admonition.

Relating the Greatest Song to the Older Testament

The "Thou shalt nots" of Exodus 20 and Deuteronomy 5 are often misunderstood as being the killjoy forbiddances of an angry authoritarian God. But such counsels are really hugs of a merciful LORD who does not want us children to get hurt. If you steal, you will be robbed of self-respect. If you murder, you will become a hunted person. Don't steal, but give things away! Don't kill, but help your neighbor stay alive!

In this way, The Song's refrain is also a solemn request, like a vow, by the virgin Shulammite to the harem women controlled by a wanton figure of authority: don't try to seduce me, keep your dirty hands off what is holy and dear to me; but let my naive, tingling corporeal desire flower into irrepressible, unspoiled joy!

The struggles throughout The Song of people imploring, disagreeing with, and confronting one another directly moves toward a resolution in the last chapter. There, the refrain's point is formulated positively:

"Hold me as a seal to your heart.
Keep me as signet ring upon your finger.
For love is as permanent as death,
and the passionate drive of love as all-consuming as the
        most terrible power.
Its flames are flashes of fire,
a pure fire of the LORD God!
Streams of water cannot put it out.
Floods of water shall never quench the fire of love.
If another man were to give all the treasures of his house
        for love,
he would be utterly despised!" (8:6–7)

The Greatest Song moves from struggle to resolution just as the books of Job and Ecclesiastes do. The nasty dialogue of Job's friends and Job's own hollering at God finally move toward God's quieting, lofty settlement of the disputes. God proclaims God's amazing creational grace by ordering the starry heavens, rain, and ferocious animals (Job 39–41). The formidable monologue of Qohelet (the main protagonist of Ecclesiastes) reflect his struggles to make sense of the success of the wicked and the failure of the righteous. The book finally ends with the positive assurance in chapter 12 that the tenuous, all-important breath of life – which keeps us mortals intact – shall indeed return to the awesome Creator God who gave it.

Similarly, in The Greatest Song the positive truth is proverbially affirmed in 8:6–7, despite all the strong temptation to succumb to forced lovemaking and the uncertainty of whether honest committed passion would be kept safe to be enjoyed.

True love is as permanent as death! The passionate drive of committed love has the consuming exclusivity of the refining fire of the Lord God. No interloper with wealth can waylay or botch such pure passion instilled and willed by God in the beginning (compare 8:6–7 to Genesis 2:21–25).

Sprinkled throughout the The Song are expressions of endearment that point to the truth of this succinct declaration on the nature of genuine human love and passion. "O, if his left hand were only under my head and his right arm holding me tight," says the Shulammite (2:6; 8:8), apprehensive of whether she will be rescued by her lover or not. It is an earthy grip on love, with its physical bodily assurance, instead of some Platonic mental conception of love.

"My lover is mine, and I am his" (2:16a; 6:3a).
"I belong to my lover! And only his passionate desire is for me!" (7:10).

Impassioned human love is mutual and singular by its very intensive nature. It involves a person wholly – *I belong* to my lover, says the Shulammite woman, and my lover *belongs wholly to me*. Because we belong together in this exclusive union of love, says the Shulammite, I want to *give* you, my lover, not only kisses but my bodily caresses, my self! (8:1b; 7:12b). Solomon doesn't belong to anybody. That is why Solomon does not know what loving is all about (8:11–12).

The physical closeness of love can bring a warm sense of safety; love is a matter of belonging, an act of giving rather than of getting. Such an awareness of the total vulnerability of love is something felt especially and emphatically by a womanly sensitivity, which we men need to hear, digest, and take to heart. Scripture is telling us this truth in the words of the Shulammite woman, reinforcing the proverbial revelation that human erotic love is as strong as death and as powerful as the jealousy of the

Lord God (a refining fire, Hebrews 12:28). Betrothed, passionate human love is meant to be for life. You are willing to die for your beloved (compare John 15:13), so tough, hardy, sacrificially strong, resilient, and enduring is true human bodily love for your betrothed partner.

Metaphor in The Greatest Song

What is worth noticing is the sensitive, delicate, and highly poetic way the Shulammite woman talks about sexual acts and the private features of her body, which the Apostle Paul calls our "members" (1 Corinthians 12:12–26). For example, the Shulammite says, her lover "delights in red lilies." She tells the daughters of Jerusalem when they ask where her lover has gone:

My lover has climbed up to his garden, to the spicy flower
     bed,
to drink in the charm of the paradise, and to gather up the
     red lilies. (6:2–3)

The Shulammite calls herself "a delicate red lily" (2:1b) in her verbal sparring with Solomon; and her lover refers to his beloved as a private garden full of lovely plants, flowers, and aromatic spices (4:12–15).

The superbly gifted writers God's Holy Spirit used to book this critique of late King Solomon's godless sensuality kept the erotic talk poetic. The shepherd lover's rapturous comments about the Shulammite as a garden of fragrant odors and a spring of bubbling flowing waters are metaphors that suggest sensuous plenitude and erotic intimacy but keep it reserved and private, filled with a not yet defined wonder. By contrast the Solomon voice says explicitly in a crude simile, "Your breasts will roll over me like clusters of grapes" (7:8b). The Shulammite keeps her talk purposely metaphoric when she exclaims to her lover how she would like to give him "a tingling wine to drink, the freshly pressed-out wine of my pomegranates" (8:2b).

A euphemism is a flowery word used as a substitute for a word that might offend fastidious people in polite society. The enigmatic "catch the foxes" (2:15) folksong melody is probably a euphemistic reference to mischievous faults or vices that harm good endeavors. A *double entendre* is using a word or phrase that can be interpreted multiple ways without clarifying which meaning is intended. Solomon's bizarre compliment that the Shulammite's teeth are like sheep "not one of which is barren, all of which will soon be bearing twins" (4:2) is a leering double entendre, hinting he will certainly get her pregnant in short order.

But a good metaphor is neither a euphemism nor a *double entendre*. Instead, a metaphor focuses on some matter in a suggestion-rich way that throws up a wonderful penumbra of meanings that make the original designation sparkle implicitly without naming the thing exactly and without spelling out the nuances. Pomegranates are a firm round, red-rosy fruit about the size of a mature breast – need the Shulammite say more? The shepherd lover shows the same elliptical soft touch: "A Paradise garden of pomegranate trees filled with choice fruits – your virgin womb is this" (4:12–13a).[1] Poetic metaphors have the lovely curve of a parabola, which never touches the literal parallel plane, making the metaphor shimmer and giving an imaginative play to the designation and calling up multiple pictorial meanings. The allusive connotations of language come to the fore in poetic expression.

The Shulammite's dream of searching for her lover in the maze of city streets, interacting with the police, finding him, and wanting to bring him home to her mother (3:1–4) is a relatively straightforward account of her subconscious anxiety. The wedding-night dream that turns into a nightmare, on the other-hand – where Solomon threatens to perfume himself to come to her and satisfy his desire (4:6b) – is awash with sexual references kept in poetic metaphors:

> I was asleep! But I was awake! – the voice of my lover? Is he knocking?!
> Open the door for me, my beloved. . . .
> But I have put off my clothes! (I said). Oh! should I put them back on again?
> My feet are already washed! Shall I go out and get them dirty again?
> My lover put his hand through the opening of the door . . .
> My senses left me at his presence, I turned all dizzy inside.
> I stood up to open the door to my lover.
> And my hands were moist with myrrh,
> my fingers were wet with myrrh on the grip of the lock.
> I opened the door to my lover –
> But my lover had turned away! He was gone!
> And I sought him without finding him! I called out to him, and he did not answer me!
> > The watchmen that go about the city saw me–
> > They grabbed me, beat me, horribly hurt me!
> > > took away my clothes–those watchmen
> > > of the [city] walls. (5:2–7)

This womanly confession to other women who are intently listening catches the uncertain tentativeness and vulnerability of nakedness and intimacy, of being elated and then disappointed, and then being beaten and hurt by strange watchmen. The Bible tells it vividly, full of unashamed sexual privacy, ecstasy, and pain, without a whiff of embarrassment *or* psychologized second-guessing. In The Greatest Song, the Bible treats sexual intercourse with great respect as a normal, primal experience to be exercised within a committed bond of love. Otherwise, the giving of yourself bodily to the other is cheapened.

That wisdom hovers over the whole book, in the tussles

between the brothers and the Shulammite, the harem and the Shulammite, the lover and King Solomon, and the Shulammite and Solomon. ". . . At our openings are the sweetest fruits," confides the Shulammite, almost to herself. "The old as well as new fruits I have kept safe, saved up for you, my lover" (7:13b). That incredibly rich, poetic line is full of wonder, mystery, and an almost secret knowledge that shouldn't be stated more plainly for fear of ruining its glorious truth. To talk of love with such frank modesty and a sure certainty reveals God's blessed hold on our individual lives. If the fruits of our openings are saved and given in an exclusive mutual jealous relationship, there will be a sweet flowing of shalom. When the red lilies of sexual identity are plucked untimely, particularly before they are ready to be given in the bond of genuine love, then something very deep in a person has been violated. The message of The Greatest Song in the Bible is:

> I plead with you,
> Never try to arouse or excite anyone's erotic passion,
> until a selfless mutual commitment of the poised lovers is
>   ready to come naturally.

Reflection

- In what ways does our culture today challenge the idea that we should save love and passion for serious commitment?

- How can we reform sex education to go beyond the medical terminology and effects of intercourse and cover the personal and relational aspects?

SUGGESTED READING: Read slowly and relate the following passages: Genesis 2:18–29, Job 2:9–10, Proverbs 5:13–23, Matthew 5:27–32, Acts 5:1–11, Ephesians 5:21–33.

6

GOD'S GIFT OF PASSIONATE, WEDDED LOVE

The Newer Testament clearly says: "All the things written earlier were put in writing for us to understand so that through the firming up and comforting power of the Scriptures we might have hope" (Romans 15:4). If there is any matter in our day on which we need comforting hope and direction, it is on the human matter of sexual desire.

Solomon's voice in The Song speaks for all the unbridled drives to get pleasure from cajoled or forced sexual submission of especially women and the young. Old King Solomon's harem, like those of rival Turkish sultans, relate directly to international human trafficking today as well as the rampant promiscuity promoted by popular culture and advertising. The word "love" has become a weasel word.

The biblical response to such sexual misery is not an ascetic ethic of repress your desires – the Older Testament does not champion monastic celibacy and abstinence. Nor does The Greatest Song encourage the Western Romantic deformation of passionate love, which encourages lovers to empathize with the purported end of ideal "true love" – tragic death (as presented in Puccini's operas or James Cameron's movie *Titanic*).

Instead, The Song celebrates the enormous sensuous pleasure women and men find in the yearning for reciprocating bodily nearness and intimacy couched in a vow of faithfulness.

The Song was and is God's way of calling all those who take up Scripture and read and hear God's voice to take joy in the process – as young Augustine of Hippo points out[1] – of desiring, of suffering, and growing in living the gift of passionate wedded love.

Love, biblically understood, is the envelope in which passionate sexual desire can develop its consuming intensity and buoy rather than harm us. Love has strength as strong as death to keep its passion jealously and exclusively committed to a helpmeet. Sexuality is such a radical and formidable gift from God because it holds the potential for us to beget and give life to a new other human being! Even in its very exercise, your sexual desire, which finds another person happy and willing to return its pleasure within a love commitment, enlarges your identity, expands who you are, and raises your creatural awareness. If a person spends one's passion without love, however, the person's residual identity is disseminated but dissipated.

God is present in The Greatest Song, revealed in the very grace embodied in the Shulammite and shepherd lover's joy in their budding, promissory erotic embraces and life together. When creatures exhibit and glory in their peculiar creatural strengths, the amazing power and wisdom of the Creator is manifest to those who have eyes to see it. And in the very climax of the book, 8:6 (although many translations of the Hebrew minimize the word YAH), the LORD God is mentioned in the poetic epigrammatic conclusion:

> "The passionate drive of love is as all-consuming as the most
> terrible power
> – its flames are flashes of fire, a pure fire of YAH, the LORD
> God."[2]

The scribes of The Greatest Song, searching for an anchor to disclose the God-willed source and God-affirmed nature of the text, dropped the word "Yah" (a shortened poetic variant of "Yahweh") into this culminating wisdom proverb. Scripture underlines the exhilarating seriousness of wedded, passionate love by positing that such a bond reminds us of the jealousy of the covenanting Lord God for God's people – wholly committed, sacrificially intense, ardent, and everlasting. But like Solomon and his harem, many people today do not understand this truth. "Why are you pleading so earnestly, O Shulammite, practically putting us under oath, not to stir up erotic passion for someone other than your committed lover?! Is he so incomparably special?" (5:9). The Shulammite proclaims, yes, erotic passion is playing with fire, and its flames of sexual love are meant to warm a single hearth!

At the heart of this commitment is marriage vows. "Hold me as a seal to your heart; keep me as a signet ring upon your finger" (8:6) acknowledges the covenanting permanence of pledging love to one another. The seriousness of the union of two humans has been recognized by many tribal societies throughout the ages with a rite of passage. It is also why some Christian communions consider wedded erotic union a sacrament. A wholehearted public marking of such a commitment, which is bodily celebrated in private, is one way to distinguish human wedded, passionate love from the copulation of animals. Humans are not rational animals, but are oath-taking creatures of a different order than the fantastic beasts of the field whom the Lord also feeds and enjoys seeing procreated (Psalm 104; Job 39).

The Female Perspective

The beloved Shulammite is treated like a tempting object by Solomon, whose admiration is made to sound fake in his outlandish, exaggerated compliments (*wasf*[3]). But the young woman is not a passive object of "the male gaze." Though captive, she is an active subject searching for her lover both in spoken enquiries (1:7; 5:8) and in her subconscious dreams (3:1–4; 5:2–7). There is a gentleness to the way her lover sings to her, "Arise, beloved, my beautiful one, come wander away with me . . ." (2:10b–13), and nothing peremptory or focused on a time-conscious rendezvous.

When asked by the harem to describe her lover, the Shulammite enthuses about his appearance in the third person (*in absentia*; 5:10–16) instead of the confrontational second person address Solomon uses in blustering about her sexualized body (to her face, 4:1–5; 6:5b–7; 7:1–9a). With curt self-assurance, the Shulammite counters King Solomon's advances (1:12; 7:9b), and puts her brothers in their solicitous place – "My breasts are as towers! and I am a virgin, chaste. Give me now your blessing!" (8:10).

The fact that the Shulammite maiden is the central character around whom both Solomon and the shepherd lover revolve, and that she has the predominant voice in The Song, lends support for us readers to consider that the God-given narrative assumes here a womanly point of view on erotic love. The Greatest Song affirms the stabilizing role of a woman in any relationship of betrothed love.

The "helpmeet" (*eser*) that God created for the man (*adam*) was not a subordinate assistant! A helpmeet can be defined as someone providing the needed safety and stability fit for the circumstances. Besides Eve, only *God* is called a "helpmeet" in Scripture.[4] It is telling that in the beginning, God said a man will leave his father and mother and *cleave to his wife* (Gen 2:24) – not the other way around! A woman is not supposed to cling to her husband, for she is the solid base of a marriage, as Proverbs 31 illustrates.[5] So it is the Shulammite who issues the invitation to her lover to come to her Edenic garden (4:13, 16b),[6] which *she* has kept safe for their coming conjugal celebration (7:13b).

The Shulammite has a good sense of what is private – amorous acts of love (2:4; 7:12) – and what is a modest show of love in public – acknowledgement of attachment (8:1–2). She is not afraid to admit to being lovesick (2:5; 5:8), languishing at the lack of her lover's embrace (2:6; 8:3). Like other strong women in the Bible – the midwives who defied pharaoh (Exodus 1:15–22), Miriam (Exodus 15:20–21), Deborah (Judges 4–5), Ruth (Ruth 1), Huldah (2 Kings 22:14–20), Esther (Esther 2,5–7), and Priscilla (Romans 16:3–4) in the Bible – the Shulammite sought the approval of her mother and brothers and the firm backing of YAH. The world of erotic love poetically explored in The Greatest Song, despite the rough vetting of lust (7:6–9a), bears overall a sunny, cheerful feel. The Shulammite and her betrothed shepherd are not star-crossed lovers, but are a woman and man whose impassioned commitment is being tested as a witness to the norm the LORD God has instituted for erotic activity. And it is the womanly emphasis upon wholesome contentment and compassionate caring in erotic intimacy, and the repeated refrain that passion is not to be hurried, that characterizes the spirit of The Song, its story, and its message.

The Stages of Love

Timing is crucial to the sound development of passionate, wedded love among men and women, which is not to say that there is a set pace at which women and men should plot the trajectory of their love. Different personalities and different cultures move at different speeds in courtship, but a person had best have an emotional self-identity fairly squared away before trying to grow the more complex erotic identity of a twosome, lest a person fracture or become emotionally dislocated. It is possibly so that one can never be completely ready to marry, since daily wedded love is not a perennial honeymoon. To prepare for the surprise, if not shock, of being united with someone else for keeps, one needs to firm up the promissory note of willing to be there for the other person for better *and* for worse.

Sexual desire for an attractive person can come easily, but wooing takes time. It is good at initial stages of flirting to be bashful. The rambunctiousness *and reticent* passion of the Shulammite and lover for each other (2:3–4; 8:1–2) honors love's decorum. After the tentativeness of flirtatious engagement, in which wonderment and affection may fail to be respected, comes the time for the two to develop a deeper bond. Shared secrets, a private vocabulary,[7] similar interests, terms of endearment ("garden," "like a gazelle") bring your respective consciousnesses closer together. Inevitably comes the bonding of physical touch, where the kissing and caresses act like pledges more sure even than the vow in words of faithful caring. The Shulammite and shepherd lover are clearly in this advanced phase of committed passion (see 2:6, 16a; 4:16b–5:1; 6:3; 7:10–13; 8:3).

When a long-range, lifelong covenantal promise of mutual jealous love matches in strength the deep-going exercise of erotic bodily passion building up between a lover and a beloved, then you may receive the intoxicating joy and pleasure celebrated by Scripture in The Greatest Song 8:6–7, Proverbs 5:18–19, and the refrain of Ecclesiastes 9:7–10. Sadly, the amazing excitement and blessing of naked wedded intimacy and union is often prohibited by the Solomonic pressure and hurry to *get* physical *gratification* (4:6b; 7:8). The Greatest Song makes it clear that humans in God's ordered world need to *give passionate love* before they can be given and receive erotic fulfillment. Unless the giving and receiving of passionate love is covenanted like the fiery jealousy of the LORD God, the marvelous mystery (as Proverbs 30:19 puts it, "of a man *in* a maid") is lost.

Because temporality is the very fabric of our mortal human nature, passionate, wedded love – once achieved – goes through stages. The lovely, romantic sunset world of the French painter Antoine Watteau makes the mistake of promoting the tempting enjoyment of the rendezvous for erotic yearning and dalliance without ever reaching married reality.[8] And troubadour songs paste on top of married love an eternal longing for fulfilled passions that frazzles into erotic fantasies. The ecstasy of youthful wedded loving does become middle-aged at some point, often seasoned by the lovers bearing children in whose lives you see your strengths and faults personified, written large.

Because none of us are wholly pure, wedded erotic love will show strains and blemishes, and passion can become suffering. Patience and forgiveness are essential to this precious gift of genuine wedded love grown old and tender. Gwendolyn Brooks' sad poem about "The Old Marrieds" gives nobility to the pathos of failing strength for loving.

> But in the crowding darkness not a word did they say.
> . . . It was quite a time for loving. It was midnight. It was
>   May.
> But in the crowding darkness not a word did they say.[9]

Shakespeare's 116th sonnet deserves the last word, since it holds up the crux of the Bible's Greatest Song on betrothed erotic love.

> . . . Love is not love
> Which alters when it alteration finds,
> Or bends with the remover to remove:
> O, no! it is an ever-fixed mark,
> That looks on tempests and is never shaken;
> It is the star to every wandering bark,
> Whose worth's unknown, although his height be taken.
> Love's not Time's fool, though rosy lips and cheeks

Within his bending sickle's compass come;
Love alters not with his brief hours and weeks,
But bears it out even to the edge of doom.[10]

Reflection

- What do you think of Daniel Lys's idea that the mention of "YAH" in The Song means we are to "live the covenant relation even in our sex life"?[11]

- Do you sense a feminine nurturing tone in The Greatest Song as distinct from a masculine combative, adventuresome tone, say, in the book of Judges or Job?

SUGGESTED READING: 1 Samuel 18–20. 2 Samuel 1, Matthew 7:1–5, John 8:1–11, Ephesians 5:21–6:4, 1 Corinthians 7:1–17

7

OTHER KINDS OF GOOD LOVE
& REDEEMING SPOILED LOVE

The Greatest Song does not consider all kinds of human love, but by celebrating wedded sexual love as it was in the beginning and by critiquing Solomon with his enormous harem, The Song is a splendid setting in which to hear Christ's startling comment on the Pharisees' judgment on divorce (Matthew 19:3–12) and the Apostle Paul's counsel on family and marital love relations (Ephesians 5:21–6:4). Also, since Scripture tells us to find new as well as old wisdom in its pages (Matthew 13:52), we would do well, in the shade of The Song, to reflect on the gift and nature of human friendship and to search our hearts on matters of sexual abuse and broken relationships.

Married love is a room in the house of God's creation that not everyone enters. Because God means it is not good for individuals to be alone (Genesis 2:28), everybody normally does begin life in some sort of family, and the Lord provides the opportunity for humans to form friendships above and beyond being somebody's neighbor. The Trinitarian God is concerned about human loneliness; this is confirmed by God's frequent and explicit word, which directs us that the crux of genuine worship is caring for orphans, widows, and widowers (Exodus 22:21–24; Psalm 146:8; James 1:27). What does The Greatest Song on love mean for those of us who do not marry, or whose romantic relationship is broken?

Human friendship is not just training for marriage but has its own, unique place, structural nature, and God-given task and blessing to offset a person's loneliness. Most friendships occur with people of the same sex especially among youth. When you are exploring who you are, it is very helpful to have a second set of eyes somewhat like yours. You can trust a friend to second-guess your intentions and actions; as quite different people, you develop a common history by spending time together. You share interests like knitting, riding bikes, camping out under the stars, or playing chess. You become more than neighbors or acquaintances; you just like one another, and it's fun to do things together. When you first leave home to be on your own – for example, as an undergraduate college student – you're at a good age and time of life to build lasting friendships.

You tell secrets to a friend. A friend criticizes your flaws and mistakes, and you good-naturedly accept the critique because loyal opposition is for your good, and sharpens up your sureness of what you want to be. You eat meals together, since tête-à-tête of relaxed communion with tasty food builds trust and confidence.

The intimacy of a mature friendship is astounding. Two friends can have a communion of fellowship infused with premonitory knowledge of the other person so thorough that fears and hopes, frustrations and joys, can be sensed by a friend almost before you are aware of it yourself. It is like having a *Doppelganger* (an identical double). Your consciousness is anticipated, resonates in, and charitably is understood, unspoken by your friend, even before you yourself can articulate what you are thinking, feeling, or wondering about. Such a longtime close friendship can become so intense, suggests Jesus in the Bible, that you might even be willing to lay down your life for a friend (John 15:13). Paul testifies that Prisca and Aquila and Epaphroditus risked their very lives for him (Romans 16:4; Philippians 2:30).

In another example, crown prince Jonathan braved being killed by his jealous father, King Saul (1 Samuel 20:24–34), to protect his friend David "whom he loved like his own life" (1 Samuel 18:1). Since Jonathan held David as dear as his own self, Jonathan made a formal covenant with David because Jonathan was willing to sacrifice his right to the kingship for David's sake (1 Samuel 18:3–4; 20:5). No wonder poet/songwriter David, in his lament at the death of Saul and Jonathan, sings:

> "I am sore distressed about you, my brother Jonathan.
> You were deeply loved by me.
> And your love for me was extraordinarily wonderful,
> surpassing the love of women." (2 Samuel 1:26)[1]

There are several things are worth noting here:

1. According to the Bible, the difference between the most devoted, developed, and durable friendship and a marriage is that the covenant of married love is consummated by two person's becoming one flesh. Committed friendship love does not come into force by virtue of physical intercourse, even if a friend is willing to lay down one's life for the friend. Friendship is a betrothed pact of trusting love, made on the simple basis of liking and having affection for the other person one has chosen, which may deepen into a sacrificing intimacy that could go beyond the love offered by a spouse.

2. Cross-sex friendship between two people in adult life is both a dangerous and a wonderful experience for married folk. While marriage is a special, sexually exclusive ordinance in God's world, a godly marriage does not ask husband and wife to renounce forming friendships, so long as the jealousy of their erotic wedded love is honored. A true friendship, where trusted intimacy is based on the friends' congeniality – they are emotionally of one mind, they are sexually at ease rather than impassioned,

they have time to complement the other's concerns – can give a married couple as individuals the room to explore new facets of God's world. A close friendship can give you room to complain and seek counsel about one's spouse, and can prevent you from both idolizing or demonizing your married life, or from having marriage and family monopolize your life.

3. Man-to-man and woman-to-woman friendships should be blessed rather than sexualized in our awareness. Scripture prompts us to talk about *homophilic* relationships. To phrase questions about "homo*sexuality*" is to poison the approach to reflection on the gift of man-to-man and woman-to-woman friendship, as if friendship be necessarily based on sexual coition, which it is not. Friendship is based on psychic affinity, on an attracted sympathy for someone who seems worthy of trust. A man-to-man and woman-to-woman friendship is God's gift as an antidote to loneliness.

Of course, you are never devoid of sexuality. You can't take off your sexuality like a suit of clothes. You are in your sexuality when you are awake or asleep, alone or in company. You stay sexed when you walk, talk, play, pray, and eat. But it's important to distinguish friendship from the relationship you have with your spouse. And just as married life is not one big sex-fest of continuous erotic intercourse, homophilic covenants *cannot*! be patterned after the exhibitionist "gay" parades of flaunting unbridled sensuality. Our oversexed-up societal universe of discourse is so distorted that some people today might even mistakenly claim that David and Jonathan's to-the-death promised friendship or John Zebedee and Jesus' special closeness – the disciple Jesus especially *loved* (John 20:2), "leaning on Jesus' bosom" (KJV, John 13:23) – were homo*sexual* liaisons.[2]

Friendship is not a physical one-flesh union that can generate children, but the committed affectional tie that binds two persons together as friends naturally involves touch. Friends touch one another too. The first time I spent two weeks speaking among a close-knit group of friends in Thessaloniki, Greece, who accepted me as one of their own, I came home to Canada and told my family, "I have kissed and been kissed and embraced by more men in two weeks than in the rest of my life!" Those kisses and bear hugs were not perfunctory, polite social greetings, but were joyful tokens of respect and closeness. We were engaged in the same absorbing, life-time consuming task of bringing imaginative grace to our neighbors. We trusted and loved one another, and were one in the Spirit. Face-to-face contact and proximity is always important to actual friendships, even if interrupted by years of separation – once in each other's presence again, the mutual attraction and loyalty is quickly rekindled.

A biblical proverb highlights the special selective, supportive availability of a good friend:

"The (genuine) friend loves you at all kinds of times;
in the most fearful straits the friend is borne to be like a
blood-brother." (Proverbs 17:17)

Redeeming Spoiled Love

In situations where family fails you or when erstwhile fair-weather "friends," multiplied by technology, abandon you, a truly reliable trustworthy friend who comes through for you is a worthy gift from the Lord:

A man or woman with (many) friends can go to pieces,
but there is a (true) friend who holds onto (you) more than
a blood-brother. (Proverbs 18:24)[3]

It is worth remembering that friendships can end without the trauma of divorce that happens with marriage. The one-flesh connection does not need to be ripped to pieces as in wedded erotic love. A friendship can end simply because one person moves far away, drastically changes in personality, or loses a foothold in the common interests. Friendships can peter out from being diluted too much – too many friends can reduce the quality time available for grounding and thriving in the vulnerable bond of self-disclosing intimacy. Money can also disturb a friendly relationship, since money tends to twist the invaluable precious giving and receiving of love and promises between persons into a measured transaction one monitors.

The worst way for a friendship to end is by betrayal: a friend who violates the trust of confidentiality has become a terrible enemy, worth cursing, as in Psalm 55:

> However, it is not a (declared) enemy who has been abusing
> me
> – that I could contend with.
> It is not a (known) adversary who has insolently misused
> me
> – then I would have hidden from him.
> But it is you! my fellow companion, my familiar trusted
> friend!
> Together we used to have sweet confidential meetings;
> we even walked with animation (together) into God's house!
> – Let desolating death break in upon such persons!
> Let them be buried alive!
> for the most despicable evils hang out and lodge deep with-
> in them. (Psalm 55:12–15)

Close friends confess to each other what lies deep in their heart. To expose such heart-deep intimacies to strangers is like being forced to be naked in public to a crowd who will jeer at your most hidden blemishes and sins, to destroy you. To become a friend makes you vulnerable, the more so as the mutual confidence deepens and enriches your lives.

When a friendship is normally ended or treacherously undone, you note or grieve its passing, and move on. Maybe in God's providing care, new friendships will appear. But what happens when abuse occurs in a family, or wedded lovers blunder and adultery murders a marriage? A child is locked permanently into a family by having the same genetic blood as the parents, and cannot get rid of that underlying connection. If a marriage is pledged to be forever, can the partners of a marriage gone to pieces be made happily whole again in love?

The Greatest Song and the Newer Testament Scriptures do not spell out in detail God's practical solution to our many-sided miseries in human love, but God's word does provide good news for victims and for violators. There are mutual responsibilities (and lapses), and *the healing Way of forgiveness and repentance* for God's adopted children who err.

In a family, not only husbands and wives are enjoined to be subject to one another, out of reverence for Christ (Ephesians 5:21, 22–33). But children and parents are both commanded to respect each other's respective desire to adhere to the mindset of Jesus Christ – doing what is right with gentle mercy (Ephesians 6:1–4).

If an authoritarian father bulldozes everybody into submission, if a mother is derelict in nurture by constantly faultfinding, or if adult children abuse their elderly parents by verbal rebellion or neglect, all in the family suffer. Wise emotional therapy, which considers a full range of historical factors, during or after such bruising ordeals can bandage the wounds and help those involved cope with their scarred lives. But it takes *grace* and a fervent patient *hope* to outlive such estrangement and, God willing, to forge a new extended familial communion of thankfulness. Integral to such renewal of familial love will be readjusting memories by *repenting* of evil done and bathing old disgruntlements with the humor of *forgiveness*.

Repentance and forgiveness are the Bible's guiding *deeds* required for redeeming broken marriages too.[4] Some marriages are a mistake of judgment; others simply remain tensed and difficult. When the vows of passionate wedded love go dead from abuse or from boredom, or are killed by unfaithfulness, the loneliness in marriage becomes insufferable. Sometimes what humans have joined together has to be *godly* cut apart. Jesus Christ lifted Older Testament "divorce laws" up out of the Jewish scribal legalistic misuse for male advantage, and proclaimed the good news: marriage is for life – that's how the Creator God set it up. Pious men commit adultery even with just their lustful eyes. Of course divorce is wrong, but the wrenching, suffering breakage of the woman and man in divorce is its own sinful punishment. It is not for others to judge (see Matthew 5:27–32; 1Corinthians 7:10–11).

When the same Pharisees brought a woman supposedly "caught in the very act of adultery" (which by their laws demanded at least two witnesses be present) and asked Jesus whether they should stone her, Jesus countered their cunning game. Jesus bent down and silently wrote with his finger in the sand.[5] And when the tormenting lawyers kept pestering him with questions, Jesus straightened up and said, "Let the one who is without sin be first to throw a stone at her." And to the sinful woman Jesus said, "I do not condemn you. Go on now, and do not commit sin anymore" (John 8:1–11).

Jesus forgives and sets the sinful free to repent – that is, to be turned from doing what is wicked and to walk humbly with God (Micah 6:8). In response to critics who want merciless payback for evil done, Jesus instructs us to relent and learn to forgive those who have trespassed against us.[6] If you do not forgive those who have done you wrong, God *cannot* forgive you *your* sins (Matthew 6:14–15).

Divorced people may never be reconciled, and abused persons may need to stay completely away from their deceivers and abusers. God does not require happy endings. Sexual sinners may cry out to God with Aurelius Augustine's searing self-incriminating plea, *Da mihi castitatem et continentiam, sed noli modo* ("O Lord, please give me chastity and continence, but not yet!").[7] God knows how our bodily passions and love can tie us up in knots and severely curse other persons, but when God gives those of us who have messed up our family or wedded love a new start, then we are *freed* to bear fruit worthy of repentance (Matthew 3:8). Some may need to live with an historical thorn in their flesh for the rest of their lives (2 Corinthians 12:7). The compassionate and merciful God, slow to anger and abounding in covenantal faithful love, still does visit generation-long reckonings upon guilty deeds (Exodus 34:6–7); but God's grace, which introduces forgiveness and opportunity to renew a spoiled life, is an extraordinary gift for many with tangled histories.

From personal experience, I know that truth. Once I became friends with a good, sensible girl who was a believer in Jesus Christ. We spent college years dating and finally became engaged. As I went away to graduate school after college, she returned to her maternal home and became a grade school teacher. During that year of separation, we developed differently and grew apart. Plans for our wedding materialized. Suddenly two months before marriage I was brought to realize I did not love her as a future lifelong partner and decided I had to break our engagement. There was general consternation among our family and friends. Only one of the several counselors I sought for advice helped me. He said, "If you don't love her, and have not slept with her, you don't have to marry her. But don't look at another girl for a year." So the young woman and I met, I soberly dissolved my promise to her, and I left for Europe and advanced study. Within a year she had happily married another man.

My understanding is that despite the despicable hurt my late consciousness of what was about to happen caused my fiancé, our parents, and our friends, I was saved from a worse action of marrying someone I did not truly, passionately love. The wise counsel to not look at another girl for a year was not penance to make reparations for a moral debt, but was to be evidence of admitting my mistake. I resolved to begin a journey to love that could be consciously responsible. The fact that after some time I was surprised by joy with a womanly helpmeet that has buoyed my life for sixty years is an unspeakable, undeserved gift worthy of The Greatest Song.

Does The Greatest Song Have Anything to Say about Singlehood?

What spills over from the constant throb of The Song is that human desire and love are called to be honest to God, playfully joyous, and fruitful. That directive also holds for those men and women who have decided not to marry. The morose comment attributed to Samuel Johnson – "Marriage has many pains, but celibacy has no pleasures" – needs to be countered by the Apostle Paul. Paul's recommendation is to stay single, as he was, if the Lord has called you to that life and you do not burn with passion for sexual satisfaction that troubled the young Augustine (1 Corinthians 7:1–9, 17).

Confirmed unmarried singles are fully human and often exceptionally richly cultured individuals who have extra time for friendships, for visiting families, and who are especially kindly open to the companionship of plants and animals. They may be singly devoted to a task that consumes all their attention and energy, such as writing books, leading a high-pressured administrative role, or embarking on a dangerous investigative journalist or missionary expedition. Some singles I know have a winsome childlike trait, a certain naive unawareness of detailed concerns that keep married folk busy. The temptation to singles is crispation, curling up in oneself, or adopting a Stoic attitude of self-sufficiency. A glory of singlehood is its possible selfless purity of service and contentment with whatever God puts on their plate (mentioned twice by Paul, a bachelor; see Philippians 4:10–14; 1 Timothy 6:6–11).

Emily Dickinson's poem catches for me the aura of a blessed singlehood:

To make a prairie it takes a clover and one bee.
One clover, and a bee,
And revery.
The revery alone will do,
If bees are few.[8]

Reflection

My own sinfulness does not excuse other people's evil deeds of betrayal, sexual abuse, or adultery. How do we call for repentance from perpetrators of evil without falling into the judgmental attitude Christ abjures (Matthew 7:1–5)?

Do you see the blessed humor in forgiveness?

8

GOD'S PRESENCE IN THE SPOKEN
BIBLICAL WORD RIGHTLY HEARD

For a reader to meet God in The Greatest Song and have their life transformed to be steady, joyful, and sorrowful (as God meant loving to be), applying the text to personal experiences is key. Here are four ways the reader might best respond to this biblical text.

As Pieces of a Puzzle

Recognize that the narrative is structured as an interlocking whole. Find its meaning by hearing its echo in the biblical canon from Genesis to Revelation – do not treat The Song as a standalone work.

The popular '60s song "His banner over me was love" picks out one piece of a verse (2:4b) and mistakes it to be referring to Christ's enveloping me with love. The reading of *The Greatest Song in critique of Solomon* I have presented shows that in this text of 2:4 the Shulammite is reveling in remembering her shepherd lover's bodily caresses, holding her close with his left arm under her head, as she now spars with a royal would-be paramour. Like literary critic John Middleton Murray tried to do when he identified "Ripeness is all" in Shakespeare's *King Lear* (V, ii), you could find one verse that serves as a theme for the whole text. You could preach an entire sermon on The Song's refrain (2:7; 3:5; 5:8; 8:4), on the summation of the whole piece in 8:6–7, or on a key repetitive sentiment (e.g., 2:16, 6:3, 7:10, 8:12) to present a message on the rightfully jealous mutuality of wedded love. But you only start to grasp the greatness of human love revealed in The Song when you read it as a single literary whole – not a collection of verses – so you get the complete biblical message of love's promise being tested in the crucible of seduction, only to be repulsed!

If you carefully and patiently reread The Greatest Song, you will notice how at the beginning of The Song the harem setting (1:1–8) and the Shulammite brothers' misjudgment, which led to her abduction, are complemented in the closing epilogue of the story (8:8–14). The initial confrontation between Solomon and the Shulammite woman in Solomon's palace (1:9–2:7) is book-ended by pronouncements of the Shulammite and shepherd lover's rejection of Solomon's advances in their rural, pastoral home (8:5–14). These recurring contrasts are evidence that The Song was composed as a unified whole.

A close reading discloses that there is a grounding section, which presents the captive Shulammite and her lover's betrothed history, desires, and wish to be reunited (including a dream, 2:8–3:5). This section serves as the mainspring for the ensuing complex, balanced, and interwoven narrative: King Solomon blatantly woos the Shulammite (3:6–4:7); then the shepherd lover sings to her his respectful yearning (4:8–5:1). The distraught Shulammite sings her fear of having the anticipated bodily union with her lover disrupted (5:2–6) and of being sexually violated by the perfumed Solomon's cohorts (5:7) (5:2–7 referring to 3:6–4:7), and then expresses her joy at being joined by her true lover (5:10–6:3 referring to 4:8–5:1). What follows is the climaxing confrontation of all the voices – Solomon, the shepherd lover, the Shulammite, and the harem (7:1–9a) – and the resolution of the conflict with Solomon's defeat and the Shulammite's reunion with her faithful lover (6:4–8:4).[1]

This passionate human love story of the Shulammite woman is told to reveal what the Almighty Lord, Creator God, fashioned for the good of men and women in the beginning (Genesis 2:18–25).[2] The Greatest Song of love resounds throughout the Scriptures in many mutations: Rebekah and Isaac's joyous love story (Genesis 24), the severe celebration of sexual holiness in Leviticus 20:10–21, the valor of judge Deborah and Kenite Jael who stood up against military evil (Judges 4–5), and the role of Rahab (Joshua 2; 6:22–25; Matthew 1:5). The Shulammite is a pearl in the necklace of renowned biblical women like Ruth, who proposed to Boaz for the sake of Naomi (Ruth 3), and Esther, whose beauty made her a Persian queen able to set in motion the rescue of her people (Esther 8).

The Shulammite and shepherd lover's commitment to one another sheds refracted light on understanding the warmth of Jesus' friendly love with Martha, Mary, and Lazarus (Luke 10:38–42; John 11:1–44); the loving hospitality of the business woman Lydia for the beaten Apostle Paul (Acts 16:14–40); and the counsel Paul gave to newly converted pagans on how to treat others as wives, husbands, children, even slaves. The reliability of human love rests in a covenantal promise of trustworthy respect and care for another person – a wedded spouse, blood relative, friend, or neighbor – and is highlighted in The Greatest Song by human desires, hopes, fear, temptations, and promises. The Greatest Song of love is a specific example of what God wills for our human lives in general (compare 1 Corinthians 13), something that the Dragon and Beasts of Revelation 12–13 do their utmost to ruin (Revelation 12:17).

As a Truthful Story

Remember to keep reading and hearing The Song in its literary idiom, as a suggestion-rich and poetically allusive but truthful way of telling us in story form what God wants us to know. The Greatest Song deals with erotic human love, but it is not a tract about sex or a theological doctrinal disquisition about God.

The imagery the shepherd lover and Shulammite use evokes the aura of caressing and enjoying bodily intimacy without reducing the matter to sexual secretions and body parts. "You are a garden," the lover says, respectfully complimenting the Shulammite, "full of choice fruits" and all kinds of the very best spices – henna, spikenard, calamus, saffron, cinnamon, aloe, and myrrh (4:12–14). "Garden" here is a metaphor, not a technical description, with the hyperbole on spices of passionate devotion, not a shopping list for aromatic ingredients! "A paradise garden of pomegranate trees filled with choice fruits – your virgin womb is this, [my beloved]" (4:13) is tender and gentle love talk. "At our openings are the sweetest fruits" (7:13) is incredibly, poetically precise without lapsing into medical terms for genitalia.

By contrast, Solomon's confrontational bluster about "*your* thighs, navel, belly, breasts, neck, eyes, nose, head, and hair" (7:1–5) has been purposely given the cold-blooded tone of someone whose whole person is lost in pornographic sexual fantasies. The Song is not being fastidious in using euphemisms instead of frank terms. Solomon's discourse has a leer to it – "soon to be bearing twins" (4:2b, 6:6b) – and the Daughters of Jerusalem are not above being sarcastic (1:8). But the Shulammite and lover's phrases – "honey and milk lie under your tongue" (4:11a) and "like a gazelle or a young deer, take me quickly away, my lover" (8:14) – bespeak delicate reticence, decorum, *promissory* passion among humans, not sex organs and emissions.

That the Bible is *God-speaking literature* always needs to be honored. That does not mean its diction should be sanctimoniously sifted through a prudish Victorian sieve. Ezekiel vehemently exaggerates the dirty whoredom of God's people with handsome young Egyptians "whose penises were as large as those of jack-asses, and whose ejaculations were like those of horses" (Ezekiel 23:20). Medical doctor Luke does not prettify the coarse speech of the charwomen with whom Christ interacted: "Blessed is the belly that carried you around, and the tits that gave you suck" (Luke 11:27).

You will go wrong if you try to read the Shulammite's marriage-night dream in The Song 5:2–7 as if it were a perfect schematic case study for a Freudian interpretation[3] and a childhood trauma was behind the fear of intercourse. There are readers who put on Lacanian[4] eyeglasses and read The Greatest Song as a carnal allegory, finding references to genitalia and mother complexes galore in the biblical text. They completely miss the chaste tone and Older Testament literary finish.[5] The traditional spiritual allegorical interpretation,[6] while consonant with the biblical matrix, relies on the theologians from the early church like Origen, Bernard of Clairvaux, and others.[7]

The root problem is that when we go to Scripture, we need to shun the mentality that believes only matters that can be formulated in simple sentences as sensible facts provide reliable knowledge. We must realize that with The Greatest Song, the Bible presents what God wants for us. God-breathed writing, which tells the truth, must be received in its literary idiom; otherwise you miss its message.

Jesus and Paul meant it literally and truly when they said that Lazarus and those who "die in the Lord" (Revelation 14:13) are sleeping (John 11:11–15; 1 Corinthians 15:12–58). Jesus Christ and the Apostle Paul are telling the metaphorical truth: as an adopted child of God, the last enemy, Death, does not kill me (John 11:25–26), since I really go as if "sleeping" to be safe and *alive* with the Lord.

As Wisdom Literature

Keep in mind that The Greatest Song fits in the genre of Older Testament Wisdom Literature, such as the Proverbs, Psalms,[8] Job, and Ecclesiastes. God used songwriters and poets, like David and Asaph (Psalm 50; 73–83) and young Solomon (1 Kings 4:32), as well as educated, literate court scribes and advisers like Isaiah, Eliakim, and Shebnah (2 Kings 18:13–19:7; 20:1–11) to put down God's word in very fine poetic form, meant to instruct God's people in living by the Lord's *torah* ("Guidelines" – Martin Buber) in daily affairs, outside rituals and sacrifices in the temple.

The mention of Tirzah (6:4) and the pronounced critique of Solomon's profligacy (8:10–11) provide strong support for the contention that God used the old counselors of Solomon, whose advice King Rehoboam rejected, to write The Greatest Song. This would help explain the back-and-forth "Yes, but . . ." character of the book and an appeal to creational ordered matters, which is normal in biblical wisdom literature.

Sometimes the question-and-answer format is explicit: "Why do you adjure us and speak so insistently about your lover?" ask the harem women (5:9). The Shulammite replies with a laudatory tribute to her lover (5:10–16), mimicking Solomon's artificial compliments. At other times the change in speaker is less oppositional: "The voice of my lover; is he coming?" questions the Shulammite to herself (2:8–10a), which is followed by two stanzas of the shepherd lover's poetic song, "Arise, beloved, my beautiful one; come, wander away with me" (2:10b–14). No wonder the Septuagint (ancient Greek translation of the Older Testament) translators, however inconsistently, designated different voices for the Hebrew text. You could expect something so negative as an expression of lust (7:1–9a) to offset the goodness of love in a piece of wisdom literature. Jesus Christ's teaching in

Matthew 5–7 certifies this dialogical format.

It is noticeable that there is no father figure in the whole book and that the mother "who gave you birth" (8:5b) is the safe authority to whom the Shulammite maiden wants to bring her lover (8:1–2). While this is not necessarily indicative of wise women counselors being involved in the writing of The Song, the pervasive vineyard metaphor, with budding vines and blossoming grapes, used instead of a plowing or agricultural metaphor also sounds somewhat feminine. It does not matter whether wise women were among those whom the Holy Spirit led to write down The Song, but it is unusual and highly significant that in the setting of a patriarchal society, a very large portion of the book is spoken by a woman, in the first person, against a fornicating man.

With an Open Mind and Heart

Finally, read The Greatest Song on your knees. Better still, listen attentively and prayerfully to The Greatest Song read aloud.

Every translation of the Bible, and every subsequent interpretation of the translated biblical text, is subjective. It cannot be otherwise, since every human is a subject acting, in action. But we subjects must submit to the object of our activity while trying not to make it into our own subjective image. Granted that the (communal) decision on what the object be is moot.

Once you recognize that The Greatest Song is a unified whole as canonically given, that it is superbly written poetic literature, and that it is a reliable historical testimony of Older Testament wise counselors, led by the Spirit, the final step is to respond to the text in keeping with its God-given nature: on your knees. Or take off your shoes as Moses did before the burning bush. Submit to what is given in holy Scripture – God speaking to you through many voices.

The Bible is also a performative text, and deserves to be spoken aloud. God is actually speaking to us in the book, not just writing to us. Even if you cannot listen with the faith of a grown-up child, if you want to receive what is given to you through the text of The Greatest Song, you will do best to *hear* The Song *spoken to* you.

We know that the Bible is meant to be read, as well. As Luke wrote, it is important that the Bible is a written document so that we (with Theophilus) might have a reliable account of what he had been orally told (Luke 1:1–4). The Apostle John wrote that he had written down enough so that we might believe that Jesus is the Messiah, the son of God, and therefore can have life in Christ's name (John 20:30–31). And the Apostle Paul quoted a proverb to the freewheeling Corinthians, reminding them not to play fast-and-easy with the Older Testament writings: "Don't go beyond what is written" (1 Corinthians 4:6).

Nevertheless, the critical fact that God's Word is reliably written does not negate the truth that for centuries the message of the Bible was transmitted orally. Moses read aloud the gracious words and injunctions God had spoken to Moses on Mount Sinai (Exodus 24:3–7). Joshua did the same before the assembled people (Joshua 8:30–35) because most of the Israelites could not read. Later, when the high priest Hilkiah found the Book of the Covenant, King Josiah had it read aloud in the temple to all the people of Judah and Jerusalem, including priests and prophets (2 Kings 22:8–23:3). The scribe Ezra too read the *torah* of Moses aloud, and Nehemiah and the Levites taught the people what the pronouncements meant (Nehemiah 8:1–12).

In Newer Testament times, the Older Testament law and prophets were read and exposited in the synagogue every Sabbath (Luke 4:16–22; Acts 13:13–16, 26–27), and the Apostle Paul's letters were read out in house church gatherings (Colossians 4:16; 1 Thessalonians 5:26–27). During medieval time biblical, handwritten manuscripts were rare treasures, and only the educated, in the largely oral culture of the day, could have access to libraries in monasteries. So the populace usually only *heard* God's word spoken upon occasions. Only after increased literacy among people and the invention of the printing press, which multiplied the writings available in print, was reading Scripture done silently.

It would be good to recapture the orality of the Bible and take seriously Paul's declaration: "So faith comes from *hearing*, and hearing through the *spoken word* of God" (Romans 10:17). The silent reading of Scripture is private and conducive to study. But the Bible is replete with storytelling narrative that begs for intonation to make the telling come alive. Language is by nature oral and aural, not visual. Speaking is essentially interactive, and sounding out God's word makes its proclamatory character clear.

I do not mean the Bible should be read aloud in an oratorical manner. The variety of Scripture should be followed in voicing its words. Compare the quiet, humble entry in Nehemiah's diary, "Remember me for good, O my God, all that I have gone through and done for this people of yours" (Nehemiah 5:19; 13:22); Pilate's flippant conversation-ending shrug, "What's truth?" (John 18:33–38); and the exuberant outburst finishing Paul's address to the church in Rome (Romans 8:31–39). And you cannot really do justice to a biblical psalm until you sing it aloud in an appropriate melody – the bitter lament of Psalm 137 as a dirge, or the paean of praise that is Psalm 150. Songs are not meant to be left on paper!

The Greatest Song (of love), in critique of Solomon, is preeminently a united chorus of voices. The biblical text is a script to be spoken and sung in concert, performed for public hearing. My presentation of The Greatest Song as a performance, freshly and literally translated from the Hebrew and arranged more than fifty years ago (1963) has been *heard* spoken and sung by many, many audiences over the years.[9] It has been well received and convincingly understood by publics in the United States, Canada, Australia, the Netherlands, Greece, and Spain. The Shulammite and shepherd lover now and then break into song, a melody composed by Swiss-Dutch cantor Ina Lohr. The Solomon figure does not sing, because Solomon does not love.

The style of performance has emphasized the spoken word, somewhat like traditional Japanese Noh theatre.[10] Visual acting is minimal, since it is the orality of the Scripture that is being brought to the fore, the vigorously interacting and opposing voices. The snap-shut cohesion of the piece, when performed, seems to make null the debate about whether or not it is a whole! Again and again the simple performance, conceived as an *oratorium* (a concert circle of prayer), has allowed the voices reciting the book to set loose the convicting power of God's presence coming through the biblical word and blessing the gritty good news about faithful love provided by the merciful, redeeming God for us human creatures.

Reflection

- Do you agree that a literary text can truly reveal God's will?
- Does using the "Yes, but . . ." method of Wisdom Literature to reveal God's directive for our lives clarify or confuse your understanding of the Bible?
- When God takes back the life breath God lent you, would you prefer people refer to you as "dead," or as "sleeping" (see John 11:11 and 11:14)?
- What would change if you started reading the Bible out loud as part of your biblical study?

9

CONCLUSION

To hear The Greatest Song spoken with conviction is like receiving manna from heaven in a wilderness of lonely people. Never try to excite or arouse erotic love until . . . it is ready, because the passionate drive of sexual desire and love is as all-consuming as the jealous fire of the Covenantal LORD God. The refrain and the climactic proverb (8:6–7) of The Song sums up its meaning. The good news is this: the sexuality of woman and man is mysteriously and deeply embedded in our creatural nature. The desire to be wholly bodily joined to one another as one body in joy and laughter is a great gift from the Creator God. Unless the woman and man are willingly, wholeheartedly committed to such all-encompassing union in a jealous vow, there will be trouble.

Solomon in all his royal glory is not worth comparing to one simple, happy bourgeois marriage celebrating its fiftieth anniversary of promises that shared good and ill in one flesh. Solomon's voice in The Song stands for the titillating blandishments of quick-and-easy sexual satisfaction, offered indiscriminately by our ubiquitous media today. Many lonely people have fallen for its lure and suffered the sting of the tempting scorpion's tail.

The shepherd lover's voice speaks of skipping through the fertile countryside as a gazelle. Singing of his beloved like an exotic garden makes their betrothed love seem like an oasis, a garden of Eden, or a promised land in a desert of exploitive lovelessness.

And the Shulammite woman's vivacious and courageous stand throughout the ordeal issues the refrain as an oath: "Do not arouse erotic love until . . . the promised troth is utterly sure and certain." As especially a woman well knows, to have one's own body entered by another person is practically a sacred act. When God who gave such an opportunity to us humans, can bless its enactment, it is time on earth for jubilation. This is the message of The Greatest Song, in critique of Solomon.

FURTHER READING

Cook, Albert. *The Root of the Things: A Study of Job and The Song of Songs* (Bloomington: Indiana University Press, 1968).

Dell, Katherine J. "What is King Solomon doing in the Song of Songs?" *Beihefte zur Zeitschrift fur die alttestamentliche Wissenschaft* 346 (2005): 8–26.

Driver, S. R. "The Song of Songs," in *An Introduction to the Literature of the Old Testament* (1897) (New York: Meridian Books, 1967), 436–453.

Estes, Daniel J. "The Song of Songs," in *Ecclesiastes and The Song of Songs*, eds. David W. Baker and Gordon J. Wenham (Downers Grove: InterVarsity, 2010), 265–444.

Exum, J. Cheryl, "How does the Song of Songs Mean? On Reading the Poetry of Desire," *Svensk Exegetisk Arsbok* 64 (1999): 47–63.

Ginsburg, Christian D. *The Song of Songs translated from the original Hebrew with a Commentary, Historical and Critical* (London: Longman, Brown, Green, Longmans, and Roberts, 1857).

Olthuis, James H. *I Pledge You My Troth: A Christian View of Marriage, Family, Friendship* (San Francisco: Harper & Row, 1975).

Pelletier, Anne-Marie. «Vue de Cantique des Cantiques, la Bible tout entière,» *L'unite de l'un et l'autre Testament dans l'oeuvre de Paul Beauchamp* (Editions Facultés jésuites de Paris, 2004), 94–118.

Seerveld, Calvin. *The Greatest Song in critique of Solomon* (Toronto: Tuppence Press, 1963, 1967, 2nd edition, 1988). See www.seerveld.com/tuppence.html

Sparks, Kenton L. "On the Song of Songs: Wisdom for Young Jewish Women," *Catholic Biblical Quarterly* 70 (2008):

277–299.

Walsh, Carey Ellen. *Exquisite Desire: Religion, the Erotic, and the Song of Songs* (Minneapolis, Fortress Press, 2000).

Waterman, Leroy. "The Role of Solomon in the Song of Songs," *Journal of Biblical Literature* 44:1–2 (1925): 171–187.

White, John Bradley. *A Study of the Language of Love in the Song of Songs and Ancient Egyptian Poetry* (Missoula: Scholars Press, 1978).

NOTES

Chapter 1: Introduction

1.   Brevard Childs, *Introduction to the Old Testament as Scripture* (Philadelphia: Fortress Press, 1979), 60.
2.   "The Greatest Song" or "The Song" is used in place of the traditional book names "Song of Songs" or "Song of Solomon" throughout.
3.   See J. F. Jacobi, *Das durch eine leichte und ungekuenstelte Erklaerung von seinen Vorwuerfen gerettete Hohe Lied,* 1772; H. G. A. Ewald, *Das Hohe Lied Salomos, 1826;* Christian D. Ginsburg, *The Song of Songs,* 1857; S. R. Driver, *An Introduction to the Literature of the Old Testament,* 1897; Leroy Waterman, *The Song of Songs,* 1948. Driver presents a very evenhanded comparison of the traditional two-character reading and the three-person interpretation in his *Introduction* (New York: Meridian Books, 1967), 437–48.
4.   See Marvin H. Pope's Anchor Bible for lengthy discussion of the varieties of the major different ways of reading this book of the Bible, *Song of Songs* (New York: Doubleday, 1977), 34–37, 89–229.
5.   *The Greatest Song in critique of Solomon,* freshly and literally translated from the Hebrew and arranged for oratorio performance (Toronto: Tuppence Press, 1963, 1967, 2nd edition, 1988).
6.   NIV adds an honest footnote about its designation of different speakers: "In some instances the divisions and captions are debatable."

Chapter 2: Historical Background

1.   According to the apocryphal book Judith, Baal-hamon was near Dothan (Judith 8:3).
2.   This is the only place in the Bible where "Shulammite" is mentioned. Marvin Pope (op. cit. 596–600) recounts the guess of

some exegetes who surmise "Shulammite" may be derived from the name "Solomon," and be a feminine name like "Solomoness." In line with his fertility cult approach to The Song, Pope himself tends to find it to be the name of a goddess intimating "peace." Pope discounts the possibility that "Shulammite" could be a variant of "Shunammite," and be referring to Abishag (1 Kings 1:4–5). If the wise counselors of Solomon whom his son Rehoboam rejected were used by the Holy Spirit to inscribe this narrative, however, it seems likely to me that "Shulammite" is an imaginative name subtly hinting at "Shunammite" and illustrating what actually took place, more than once, in Israel's early monarchy, and that God was displeased at such activity.

Chapter 3: Biblical Wisdom Literature and Telling True Stories

1. The RSV and NRSV translate the Hebrew *ru'ah* of Proverbs 1:23 as "thoughts," but the NIV uses the word "heart." In my opinion, the King James translation is correct in using "spirit." The voice of Wisdom in Proverbs 1 promises to pour out "my Spirit" upon those who stand in awe of the Lord. In my judgment, "Wisdom" with a capital "W" is an Old Testament reference to God's Holy Spirit. See Genesis 41:38–40; Exodus 31:1–5; Isaiah 11:1–3; Daniel 5:1–12.

2. Joseph fit into the very old tradition of Egyptian "wise men," like Ptah-hotep, c. 2500 BC. See *The Ancient Near East: An Anthology of Texts and Pictures*, ed. James Pritchard (Princeton University Press, 1958), 234–237.

3. Interpreting dreams was the province of "the wise."

4. See C. Seerveld, "The Imaginative 'Yes, but' Pedagogy of 'the Wise,' and the Literary Configuration of Proverbs 1–9," in "Proverbs 10:1–22: from Poetic Paragraphs to Preaching" (1998), in *Biblical Studies & Wisdom for Living*, ed. John H. Kok (Sioux Center: Dordt College Press, 2014), 111–115.

5. See Acts 19:13–20.

---

6. See Matthew 12:28.
7. The seven more tricky evil spirits would be self-righteous ones!
8. See Mark 9:25; 2 Peter 2:20–22.
9. Yes, some of this language is obnoxious, but notice how Jesus deals with it. Bible readers today often miss a sense of the coarse populace Jesus contended with; his milieu was not genteel middle class. The King James Authorized translation of μαστοὶ uses a term few today would recognize: "paps."
10. Compare this entire passage (Luke 11:14–28) to Matthew 12:22–30, Mark 3:19b–27.
11. Marvin Pope's learned conjecture from Ugaritic parallels demonstrates the contortions scholars can go through to avoid accepting the canonic text given us; cf. his *Song of Songs*, 558–560.

Chapter 4: Contrasting Tenor of Opposing Voices on Love

1. With Bernard Boyd, "A Song about Dodai" (Chapel Hill: University of North Carolina, no date, mimeograph 17 pages), I propose a textual vowel variant in 5:9: מִדְּוִד for BH מִדּוֹד to highlight the harem rationale for their existence: give birth to a child in the line of David!
2. A corroborating judgment by Scott B. Noegel and Gary A. Rendsburg help take the dating (c. 900 BC) and place name seriously. "The twenty grammatical and thirty-one lexical items delineated above demonstrate that the Song of Songs is a northern composition" (52). We see the "Aramaic and MH parallels not a sign of lateness but as indications of northernness" (54), in *Solomon's Vineyard: Literary and Linguistic Studies in the Song of Songs* (Atlanta: Society of Biblical Literature, 2009).

Chapter 5: A Godly Nugget of Wisdom

1. As the NRSV footnote to 4:13 says, the Hebrew שְׁלָחַיִךְ is uncertain. I follow the Zürcher Bibel with (*Schoss*) "Womb," since the word is metaphorically laden. KJV and NIV "plants," RSV and JB "shoots" are opaque. NRSV "channel" takes a possible option.

Buber's circumlocution is fascinating: "Was dir sich entrankt" (what bewaters/fructifies/fecundates you).

Chapter 6: God's Gift of Passionate, Wedded Love

1. *Confessions*, VIII, 3.

2. Regarding שַׁלְהֶבֶתְיָה (*shalhevet Yah*) in 8:6, the KJV and RSV make do with "a most vehement flame." NIV translates "like a mighty flame" with a footnote "Or / *like the very flame of the Lord*." JB has "a flame of Yahweh himself." Zürcher Bibel, "wie Flammen des Herrn," and Buber, "eine Lohe oh von Ihn her!" Paul Ricoeur agrees with Beauchamp's judgment that if readers take "YAH" as a strong adjective rather than as a poetic reference to the Lord God's jealous covenantal love, one has missed the capstone significance of this concluding passage and its tie-in to Wisdom; see André LaCocque and Paul Ricoeur, *Thinking Biblically: Exegetical and Hermeneutic Studies*, translated David Pellauer (University of Chicago Press, 1998), 300 n.39.

3. A *wasf* is an old Syrian elaborate, even exaggerated, description in detail of a female or male physical appearance. Its role in Arabic *tašbib* and *hijā'* poetry is debated. See Noegel and Rendsburg's exhaustive discussion, op. cit. 129–169.

4. Cf. Exodus 18:4; Deuteronomy 33:7; 2 Kings 14:26; Psalms 33:20; 46:1; 115:9–11; 121:2; 124:8; 146:5.

5. The metaphor my wife and I settled on during our first year of marriage was this: the umbrella. The wife usually is the pole, which holds up the whole ensemble, and the husband is the covering material, which is first for the rain or snow to hit. Cf. C. Seerveld, "From Systemic Suppression of Women to Asymmetrical Gender Mutuality: An historical and systematic introduction" (2006) in *Cultural Problems in Western Society,* ed. John H. Kok (Sioux Center: Dordt College Press, 2014), 105–28.

6. Cf. 4:11, which states "(as if) honey and milk lay under your tongue," is an echo of "the Promised land" mentioned in Exodus 3:8, 17; 13:5; 33:3; Numbers 13:27; and Deuteronomy 26:9, 15.

7. "Catch the foxes" (2:15) is possibly just a little folk tune that the

lovers use to signal their close whereabouts. It is not an occasion for theological doctrines or moral lessons, which it has been interpreted as.

8. Cf. C. Seerveld, "Telltale Statues in Watteau's Painting," (1982) in *Art History Revisited,* ed. John H. Kok (Sioux Center: Dordt College Press, 2014), 171–95.

9. Gwendolyn Brooks, "The Old Marrieds," in *The Poetry of Black America: Anthology of the 20th Century*, ed. Arnold Adoff (New York: Harper & Row: 1973), 154.

10. William Shakespeare, "Sonnet 116," lines 2–11, accessed 6 March 2017, https://www.poets.org/poetsorg/poem/let-me-not-marriage-true-minds-sonnet-116.

11. Daniel Lys, *Le plus beau chant de la creation: Commentaire du Cantique des cantiques* (Paris: Éditions du Cerf, 1968), 52.

Chapter 7: Other Kinds of Good Love

1. Background for David's remark might have been his experience with polygamous marriage, since he had six wives before he seduced Bathsheba, and his married life probably was not all roses. Wife Michal, for example, both saved his life (1 Samuel 19:8–17) and later mocked his boisterous public dancing before the ark of the Lord (2 Samuel 6:12–23).

2. The Greek φιλέω (*phileō*; friendly love) and ἀγαπάω (*agapaō*; wholehearted selfless love) are used loosely in many English Bible translations as simply "love." Only John refers to himself as "the disciple whom Jesus loved" (*ēgapa* [John 19:26, 21:20] and *ephilei* [John 20:2]) to distinguish himself neatly from Simon Peter. In my judgment, when asking Peter whether Peter *"agapas* me"? (Do you wholeheartedly selflessly love me?), after hearing Peter say, *"philo* you" (I am truly your friend): when Jesus the third time asks "*phileis* me"? (Are you truly my friend, Peter?), it really breaks Peter's heart, who still responds with *phileō*, "My Lord, you know everything, you know firsthand that I truly . . . am your friend" (John 21:15–17). Even though you are not John, says Jesus to Peter in conclusion – John is reporting this conver-

sation! – follow me anyhow, Peter. My followers have different kinds of "love" for me I am glad to accept and bless with grace.

3.   Martin E. Marty's clever quip is apropos: "What a Jesus we have in a friend." *Friendship* (Allen: Argus Communications, 1980), 117.

4.   Rudolph Bultmann emphasizes that "forgiveness" is not an "idea" of God but is veritably a *deed* God has done to redeem us humans who repent, so we may follow through by forgiving others. Cf. article on ἀφίημι, in *Theologisches Worterbuch zum Neuen Testament*, ed. Gerhard Kittel (Stuttgart: W. Kohlhammer, 1933) 1:507–09.

5.   See Kenneth E. Bailey's convincing supposition that the phrase "*kill her*" is what Jesus wrote in the sand, so as not to violate the Pharisaic interpretation prohibiting work on the "sabbath," and so as not to disturb the peace enforced by watching Roman soldiers, in Kenneth E. Bailey, *Jesus through Middle Eastern Eyes: Cultural Studies in the Gospels* (Downers Grove: InterVarsity, 2008), 227–38.

6.   Matthew 7:1–5; John 7:14–24; cf. Proverbs 25:21–22.

7.   *Confessions*, VIII, 17. Translated by the author.

8.   Emily Dickinson, "To make a prairie it takes a clover and a bee," in *Poems*, eds. M.L. Todd and T.W. Higginson (Boston: Roberts Brothers, 1890), 1895.

Chapter 8: God's Presence in the Spoken Biblical Word Rightly Heard

1.   Cf. J. Cheryl Exum, "A Literary and Structural Analysis of the Song of Songs," in *Zeitschrift fur die Alttestamentliche Wissenschaft* 85 (1973): 47–49. I see the adjuring refrain as an ending, not as the beginning of a pericope.

2.   Karl Barth, *Die Kirchliche Dogmatik*, III,1, *Die Lehre von der Schopfung* (Zollikon-Zürich: Evangelische Verlag, 1945), 357–361, and Phyllis Trible, chapter 5 in *God and the Rhetoric of Sexuality* (Philadelphia: Fortress Press, 1978), and Paul Ricoeur,

"The nuptial metaphor" in André LaCocque and Paul Ricoeur, *Thinking Biblically: Exegetical and Hermeneutic Studies*, translated David Pellauer (University of Chicago Press, 1998), all relate The Greatest Song to Genesis 2.

3. Sigmund Freud (1856–1939) developed a psychoanalytic treatment that explained many adult neuroses as being defensive outcroppings of childhood sexual trauma.

4. Jacques Lacan (1901–1981) was a French Freudian psychoanalyst philosopher who altered and complicated Freudian categories with forays into feminist and linguistic symbolics.

5. Roland Boer uses his Lacanian-Marxist reading glasses to interpret The Greatest Song; cf. Part 1 in *The Earthy Nature of the Bible: Fleshly readings of Sex, Masculinity, and Carnality* (Basingstoke: Palgrave Macmillan, 2012). As Fiona C. Black would put it, Roland Boer's analysis "says more about the interpreter's sexual interests than anything else" (40), in "What is my Beloved? On Erotic reading and The Song of Songs" in *The Labour of Reading: Desire, Alienation, and Biblical Interpretation*, eds. Fiona C. Black, Roland Boer, Erin Runions (Atlanta: Society of Biblical Literature, 1999), 35–52. Chana Bloch notes that expositors of The Song can fail if their responses do not find "the proper register in English," in "Translating Eros," in *Scrolls of Love: Ruth and the Song of Songs,* eds. Peter Hawkins and Lesleigh Cushing Stahlberg (New York: Fordham University Press, 2006), 154. Cf. C. Seerveld, "Overlooked Herder, and the Performative Nature of שיר השירים as Biblical Wisdom Literature," *Southern Theological Review*, 4/2 (Winter 2013): 210–12.

6. The explanatory notes throughout The King James English translation refer to "The Church's love unto Christ." Cf. also Christopher W. Mitchell's present day magisterial *Concordia Commentary* (St. Louis, 2003, 1343 pages!), which, after twenty-six years of study, interprets The Greatest Song in a bold (Lutheran) Christological way, to be about "divine love." In my judgment Paul Ricoeur's intra-biblical, intertextual metaphorical approach opens up a much more intelligible and rewarding reading "than

that of Platonizing allegorism conceived of as the vertical transfer from the sensible to the intelligible, at the risk of abolishing, denying, even of defaming the sensible" (op. cit., 301).

7.   Marvin Pope details how Church proponents of an allegorical reading of The Greatest Song interpreted the book from Origen through John Wesley. Op. cit., 112–32.

8.   For example, Psalms 1; 37; 39; 49; 73; 112; 119; 127; 128; 133; 139.

9.   Calvin Seerveld, *The Greatest Song in critique of Solomon* [1963, 1967] (Toronto: Tuppence Press), 2nd edition, 1988. www.seerveld.com/tuppence.html

10. Theologians who dismiss "the dramatic" interpretation of The Greatest Song need to consider the alternative. The semi-ritual presentation of Japanese Noh theatre is close to the "Yes, but . . ." tension of biblical wisdom literature with opposing voices (like Job), but is a far cry from the action-based drama genre of Shakespeare. "Though the Song is not a drama . . . it is dramatic in effect," note Ariel and Chana Bloch, *The Song of Songs: A New Translation with an Introduction and Commentary.* Afterword by Robert Alter (New York: Random House, 1995), 16.

Appendix

The Greatest Song

Translation by Calvin G. Seerveld from *The Greatest Song*
(Tuppence Press, 1967/1988©).

(First rhapsody – as Solomon passes through the harem.)

1:1
CHORUS OF VEILED WOMEN

^{2} O! If he would only soak me with the passionate kissings
of his mouth!

SOLO VOICE

– your caresses are so much more intoxicating than wine . . .

ANOTHER

^{3} – aroma of your salves hangs sweet in the air . . .

ANOTHER

– your very name is soothing like oil poured [upon the
body – Solomon . . .]

ANOTHER

– that is why young women fall in love with you.

SHULAMMITE GIRL [enters, looking back . . .]

^{4} Take me by the hand along with you again – hurry! [my
lover!]

The king has brought me into his bedrooms!

HAREM CHORUS

We shall exult and celebrate it with you! Let us drink!

"Your kisses are more intoxicating than wine" – Everyone
who desires you is worthy, [O King!]

SHULAMMITE

[5] I am blackened but I am comely, daughters of Jerusalem,
dark as the tents of Kedar, dark as the rich tapestries of
Solomon!

[6] Do not look at me because I am so dark, burned brown
by the sun.

My brothers were infuriated at me and made me guard the
gardens –

My own garden I have left unguarded . . . .

[7] Tell me aloud, my lover, where you are wandering, where
shall you lie [in the grass] this noon?

Why should I be a veiled woman in this herd of your
bedfellows?

A LEADING HAREM WOMAN

[8] If you do not know [anything], my most beautiful woman,
Get out and follow the sheep herds; feed your goats around
the huts of the shepherds.

SOLOMON

[9] You remind me of my war horse in the chariot from
Pharaoh, my lovely one.

[10] How beautiful your cheeks will be [half-hidden] in
plaited [hair]!

How beautiful your neck will be with a string of red and
green coral shells!

[11] Chains of gold with ornaments of silver will be hammered
out for you –

SHULAMMITE

[12] When the king was in his harem house, my source of
fragrance was spilling out of its sweetness.

[13] My lover['s head] lay between my breasts like a little
pouch of myrrh.

[14] A cluster of henna blossoms was my lover to me, found in

the gardens of Engedi.

SOLOMON

[15] Yes, you are well formed, my lovely one, very pleasantly formed,

And your eyes are as innocent as a dove . . .

SHULAMMITE

[16] My lover is well formed! even wonderfully formed . . .
Our bed is a bed of fresh growing flowers –

SOLOMON

[17] The beams of our houses are made of well-cut cedar and the rafters are fashioned from Phoenician juniper trees.

SHULAMMITE

[2:1] [But] I am a wild flower from the Sharon plains, [he said,] a delicate red lily from the plain country.

SOLOMON

[2] Yes, you are like a lily, a lily next to – thistles!

That is what you are, my lovely one, compared to the daughters [of Jerusalem].

SHULAMMITE [reflecting almost to self, as some harem women quietly return and listen:]

[3] My lover is like an apple tree deep in the woods, an apple tree compared to other young men.

How I longed to go sit in his shadow; his fruit was always so sweet in my mouth.

[4] He would lead me out to a [hidden] arbor, and cover me there with his love.

[5] Help me! Give me something to eat! Freshen me with – apples! For I am lovesick. . . .

[6] O, if his left arm were only under my head and his right arm holding me tight –

[7] Daughters of Jerusalem! I plead with you – do you not

know the gazelles and the hinds of the plain country?
I plead with you,
Never try to arouse or excite a beloved! till the love come
naturally.

(Second rhapsody. It is now morning, the Shulammite is alone on a couch in a small room; suddenly attent.)

SHULAMMITE

[8] The voice of my lover – ? Is he coming?!

tripping along the mountains skipping over the hills
[9] like young deer or gazelles – so runs my lover.
There he is!

outside our walls, looking in at the windows, trying to
peer through the shutters.

[10] He has answered [my call]! My lover! – there he is –
singing to me!

HER LOVER

"Arise, beloved, my beautiful one.
Come wander away with me.
[11] *The winter is past; the heavy rains gone;*
[12] *New flowers shoot forth from the earth,*
The turtle dove coo is heard.
[13] *The fig tree colors its unripe fruit;*
All vines are bursting with buds – O! the fragrance.
Arise beloved, my beautiful one
Come wander away with me.
[14] *In the clefts of the rock,*
In the lonely heights of the mountains,
I always hoped to see you appear and strained to hear you
singing,
For your voice is sweet and countenance so lovely . . .
Arise, be loved, my beautiful one,
Come wander away with me.

SHULAMMITE *(singing a ditty they used to sing together)*
[15] *Catch the foxes. Catch the little foxes*

Which ruin the grapes and gardens,
For our vineyards are now in bloom.
Catch the foxes. Catch the little foxes. Ah –

[16] My lover is mine and I am his – He who delights in red lilies.

(Harem women come, awakened by her singing:)

[17] Turn away! my lover.

[Run] like the gazelle or a young deer to the sweet-smelling mountains,

till the day fade away and the shadows [of night] creep out . . .

[3:1] During the night, while sleeping, I felt as if my lover were there.

I tried to reach – but could not grasp him. [2] I will get up, [I said,] I must embrace him.

Into the city, down the streets and alleys, I will pursue the love of my heart.

I tried to catch him, but could not find him!

[3] The watchmen who go about throughout the city discovered me.

Have you seen my lover?" [I asked,]

[4] But scarcely had I passed them by than I found him!

I clutched the lover of my heart and would not let him go,

not till I had brought him to the home of my mother,

to the bedchamber where I was conceived.

[5] Daughters of Jerusalem! I plead with you – do you not know the gazelles and hinds of the plain country? I plead with you,

Never try to arouse or excite a beloved – till the love come naturally.

(Third rhapsody. The Shulammite, now veiled, disconsolately passing time with the women in the harem:)

ONE OF THE WOMEN

[6] What is that coming up out of the distant grasslands surrounded by columns of smoke from torches, perfumed by burning myrrh and frankincense and all kinds of foreign spices?

ANOTHER

[7] Look! It is the traveling couch of Solomon!

Sixty mighty men surround it, sixty of Israel's heroes,

[8] Each man gripping a sword, experienced in battle,

Each man with a sword on his thigh to keep away fear in the night.

ANOTHER

[9] King Solomon has made this litter from Lebanon wood!

[10] Its poles are made of silver! Its cloths of support are made of gold!

Its sitting place is purple-covered! Inside it is fitted out for – love-making . . .!

ANOTHER WOMAN

Daughters of Jerusalem! [11] Come out! Daughters of Zion! Come see King Solomon

crowned with the crown his mother gave him on his wedding day!

SOLOMON (enters the room, and the harem withdraws)

[4:1] Come here, my lovely one.

You are pleasantly formed, very pleasantly formed.

Your eyes are as innocent as a dove behind your veil.

Your hair [floats as gently] as a herd of goats wending its way down Mt. Gilead.

[2] Your teeth [shine out] like a flock of sheep newly shorn coming up out of their watering place

    – not one of which is barren, all of which will be bearing
        twins –

[3] Your lips are like a red ribbon. Your mouth is so pretty.
Your temples are like a piece of pomegranate [hidden]
        behind your veil.
[4] Your neck [stands majestic] like a tower of David built for
        battle,

        where a thousand shields might be hung, all of them
        shields of heroes!
[5] Your breasts are like two little fawns, twins of a gazelle,
        which feed among the lilies. . . .

SHULAMMITE

    [6] – till the day fade away and the shadows [of night] creep
        out!

SOLOMON

    I will wait in a mountain of myrrh and in hill[s] of
        frankincense!

    [7] All of you is very pleasantly formed, my lovely one, not a
        blemish anywhere.

(Fourth rhapsody. Early evening has come; the Shulammite is alone, dozing
    fitfully – dreaming; but starts awake as the song comes nearer.)

HER LOVER

    [8] *Come away with me from that Lebanon, my bride.*
    Come away with me from that Lebanon.
    Come down from that inaccessible thicket of Amana.
    Come down from that snow-clad top of Mt. Shenir and
        Hermon.
    Come out of that den of lions.
    Come out of those leopard caves!

(Her lover pauses; climbs nearer to the Shulammite's window.)

    [9] You make my heart beat hard, my bride, my sister.

You make my heart beat stronger with just one glance of
     your eyes,

     by a single movement of your throat.

[10] How lovely is your love, my bride, my sister.

How much more gently flowing is your love even than
     wine,

     and the odors of your oils are sweeter than the scent of
     any balsam.

[11] O, my bride! Your words fall soft like drops of honey,

     [as if] honey and milk lay under your tongue,

     and the smell of your clothes is as fragrant as the
     shrubs of Lebanon,

[12] A garden! –

A garden closed off,

A well covered over,

A fountain sealed tight – is my bride-to-be

[13] A paradise garden of pomegranate trees filled with choice
     fruits – your virgin womb is this, [my beloved].

[You are an untouched garden] of blooming henna bushes
     and spikenard plants, [14] of calamus and saffron
     flowers, of cinnamon and Indian aloe trees, all kinds
     of incense trees, [with the air full of] nard and myrrh
     and the very best spices –

[15] *A garden!*

A spring of bubbling waters flowing down from Mt. Lebanon.

SHULAMMITE

[16] *Wake up, North Wind! Come here, South Wind!*

Blow through my garden and waft its spicy odors

That my lover may come to his garden and taste its sweet fruits.

     Ah –

HER LOVER

[5:1] *I come to my garden, my bride-to-be.*

I gather my myrrh and spice.

I taste of the honey in my honeycomb,

And drink deep of the wine and the milk.

(Interruption; the harem women come to deck the Shulammite for the bridal night. Flustered, she turns away from the window in consternation.)

HER LOVER

Eat and drink, my friends! Get drunk with your lovemakings!

SHULAMMITE

2 I was asleep! But I was awake! – the voice of my lover!? Is he knocking?!

Open the door for me, my beloved, my sister, my dove, my beautiful one!

[Open the door for me, I thought I heard him say,]

For my head is covered with dew, and my hair is damp with moisture of the night.

3 But I have put off my clothes! [I said] – Oh! Should I put them back on again?!

My feet are already washed! Shall I go out and get them dirty again?

4 My lover put his hand through the opening of the door . . .

My senses left me at his presence, I turned all dizzy inside.

5 I stood up to open the door to my lover.

And my hands were moist with myrrh, my fingers were wet with myrrh on the grip of the lock.

6 I opened the door to my lover –

But my lover had turned away! He was gone!

And I sought him without finding him! I called out to him, and he did not answer me!

7 The watchmen that go about the city saw me – They grabbed me, beat me, horribly hurt me! and took away my clothes – those watchmen of the [city] walls.

⁸ Daughters of Jerusalem! I plead with you – if you should find my lover –

but what could you tell him!? – [tell him] I am love sick. . . .

A HEAD WOMAN OF THE HAREM

⁹ But what is your lover compared to [the line of] David, most beautiful woman?

What is your lover compared to [the line of] David! that you should speak so insistently [about him] to us?

SHULAMMITE

¹⁰ My bronze and ruddy lover is one in a thousand!

¹¹ His head stands out like the finest gold, and his shock black raven hair shakes loose all [around it].

¹² His [gentle] eyes look out as peacefully as a pair of doves washing themselves in milk at the edge of a running brook.

¹³ His cheeks are a bed of perfume, a retreat of sweet-smelling herbs.

His lips like red lilies trickle drops of myrrh.

¹⁴ His arms [flash] like rolls of gold set with precious stones from Tarshish.

His [hard flat] belly is an art work in ivory covered over [as it were] with white sapphires.

¹⁵ His [sturdy] legs are marble pillars built on gold foundations.

His appearance as a whole is more striking than the greatest cedars of Mt. Lebanon.

¹⁶ His mouth – his kisses are a ravishing sweetness!

All of him is altogether precious?

This is my lover! So is my man!

Daughters of Jerusalem!

ANOTHER HEAD WOMAN OF THE HAREM

[6:1] Where has your lover gone, most beautiful woman?

To where has your lover turned away? so that we may search for him with you?

SHULAMMITE

[2] My lover climbed up to his garden, to the spicy flower bed,

To drink in the charm of the paradise, and to gather up the red lilies.

[3] *I belong to my lover*
And my lover belongs to me.
He is the one, the only one,
Who shall gather in the red lilies. Ah —

(Fifth rhapsody. The women have dressed the Shulammite. Solomon comes stately in to get the new bride.)

SOLOMON

[4] My! You have been dressed well, my lovely one;

You are as pleasantly clad as Tirzah, as beautiful as Jerusalem
– frighteningly impressive!

[5] [What is it?!] Do not look at me so! Your eyes disturb me. . . .

Your hair [floats as gently] as a herd of goats wending its way down Mt. Gilead.

[6] Your teeth are like a flock of mother sheep coming up out of their watering place
– all soon to be bearing twins, not a one barren.

[7] Your temples are like a piece of pomegranate [hidden] behind your veil.

(Suddenly, a ringing young voice penetrates into the room from beyond the window. The Shulammite stands transfixed.)

HER LOVER

[8] King Solomon has sixty queens, eighty concubines, and a hoard of young girls!

[9] This one only is mine, this innocent dove – my beautiful

one!

This is the only daughter of her mother, her favorite child!

Women have seen her and always marveled; even the queens
and concubines have praised her –

CHORUS OF HAREM WOMEN

[10] Who is that just visible out there?!

[Who is that shining] down so red in the morning sky?
handsome as the moon, brilliant as the sun, majestic as
the glowing planet in the sky?!

(Solomon, irate, dispatches guards to catch the trespasser; the harem
women begin to rush out of the room too, but then wait as the
Shulammite speaks – to Solomon.)

SHULAMMITE

[11] [The other day] when I went down to the grove of walnut
trees to see the budding flowers by the brook, to see
whether the vines had burst into blossom and the
pomegranates were abloom,
[12] before I knew it, you [O King,] had had me set fast
in the royal traveling couch. [I will away!! –]

(She turns her back on Solomon, forlorn, but determined.)

CHORUS OF HAREM WOMEN

[13] Turn around, turn around, oh Shulammite!

Turn around, turn around, so we can see you!

SHULAMMITE

What do you want to see in "the Shulammite"!

The sword dance of the bride from Mahanaim?

(At this outburst the women withdraw; the Shulammite breaks into crying;
Solomon watches, but determined to win her, begins again his
advances.)

SOLOMON

[7:1] How elegant is your walk in those [new] shows, "Royal

Daughter"!

The curve of your thighs is a womanly ornament fashioned by the hand of a master artist.

[2] Your navel is like a little round cup and needs to be filled with spicy wine.

Your belly is like a [shimmering] mound of wheat encircled by lilies.

[3] Your breasts are like two little fawns, twins of a gazelle.

[4] Your [lovely] neck is a tower of ivory.

Your eyes are [as deep as] the pools near Heshbon, at the gates of that great city.

Your nose is like the tower of Lebanon which looks out toward Damascus.

[5] Your whole head is as stately as Mt. Carmel.

Your [tantalizing] hanging locks of hair glisten dark
   – a king! is caught in those tresses.

[6] How wellformed, how pleasantly formed you are –
   beloved! –

compared to the most delightfully enchanting things.

[7] Your flowering figure reminds me of a palm tree, your breasts are like clusters of dates –

[8] I said to myself, I will go climb the palm tree! I will go grab hold of its date clusters!

Your breasts will roll over me like clusters of grapes;

The breath of your nose will fill me like the smell of [ripe] apples;

[9] Your kisses will flow like sweet wine –

(As he goes to raise her veil, the Shulammite, shamed at such language, righteously angry, breaks away, cuts him off witheringly.)

SHULAMMITE

   – Wine flowing straight to mouth of only my lover!
      not touching at all such well-worn lips!

[10] I belong to my lover! And only his passionate desire is for me!

– 103 –

(At his moment the guards enter with her lover; and the harem women crowd in behind.)

[11] My lover! Let us go away, back to the open plain country! Let us go spend the nights among the henna blossoms.
[12] Let us go visit the gardens early, early in the morning, to see

whether the vines have burst into blossom,

whether the budding flowers have opened up,

whether the pomegranates have come to a bloom.

There I will give you my caresses:
[13] the apples of love bear a misting fragrance, and at our openings are the sweetest fruits –

The old as well as new fruits I have kept safe, saved up for you, my lover!

[8:1] O! if you were only a brother that sucked the breasts of my mother, I would cover you with kisses here in public now that I have found you, and no one could think me immodest!

[2] O! if I could only lead you [immediately] to the home of my mother who brought me up, [then] I would give you a tingling wine to drink, the freshly pressed-out wine of my pomegranates!

[3] *O, if his left hand were only under my head and his right arm holding me tight – Ah!*

[4] Daughters of Jerusalem! I charge you –!

Why did you try to arouse and excite a beloved before the love came naturally?

(Solomon turns and leaves the room with his guards.)

(Final rhapsody: The troubled brothers of the Shulamite stand about, near one of the vineyards that they had made her guard alone.)

THE ELDEST BROTHER
[5] Who is that there coming up out of the distant grasslands,

leaning upon her lover?

(The Shulammite and her lover approach the orchard, in sight, but not in hearing of the brothers.)

THE LOVER

It was under [that] apple tree I first woke you up [to love, my beloved],

[at home] there where your mother gave you birth.

(They move to the spot and take, or renew as it were, their marriage vow, facing each other.)

THE LOVER

⁶Hold me as a seal to your heart;

SHULAMMITE

Keep me as a signet ring upon your finger.

THE LOVER

For love is as permanent as death,

SHULAMMITE

And the passionate drive of love as all-consuming as the most terrible power!

THE LOVER

Its flames are flashes of fire —

SHULAMMITE

A pure fire of the LORD God!

THE LOVER

⁷Streams of water cannot put it out;

SHULAMMITE

Floods of water shall never quench the fire of love.

THE LOVER

If an other man were to give all the treasures of his house for love?

SHULAMMITE

He would be utterly despised.

(They move to where her brothers are congregated.)

SHULAMMITE

⁸ [Long ago by brothers said,] Our little sister has no breasts,

[But] what shall we do for our sister when the lovers begin to come?

⁹ If she be modestly chaste, we shall set upon her [head] a crown of silver;

But if she would dally with them all, we will barricade [the way] to her with planks of wood.

¹⁰ My breasts are as towers! And I am a virgin, chaste.

I am come now before them to await [their] blessing.

HER LOVER

¹¹ Solomon has a [huge] vineyard in Baal-Hamon and has placed others in charge to watch it –

For its fruits men must pay a thousand pieces of silver!

¹² The thousand are yours, [King] Solomon, and may the watchmen [of your walls] have hundreds!

My [single] vineyard here before me is for me alone.

¹³ O! [beloved!] you who are so at home in the lovely gardens,

all the people here are waiting to hear your voice – let me hear it too!

SHULAMMITE

¹⁴ *Like the gazelle or a young deer,*

Take me quickly away, my lover,

Out to the sweet-smelling mountains.

Calvin Seerveld is Senior Member in Philosophical Aesthetics emeritus at the graduate Institute for Christian Studies in Toronto, Canada. He was taught Hebrew at Basel University, Switzerland (1955–56), and studied Older Testament theology in Heidelberg with Gerhard von Rad and Claus Westermann (1966–67). Biblical Wisdom literature is his hobby. *Biblical Studies & Wisdom for Living* (Dordt College Press, 2014), *Voicing God's Psalms* (Eerdmans, 2005).